FOOTBALL'S BEST OFFENSIVE PLAYBOOK

Dwight "Dee" Hawkes, MS
Hawkes & Associates, Inc., Bothell, WA

Editor

Human Kinetics

Library of Congress Cataloging-in-Publication Data

Hawkes, Dwight, 1936-
    Football's best offensive playbook / Dwight "Dee" Hawkes.
        p.   cm.
      ISBN: 0-87322-574-0
      1. Football--Offense.   2. Football--Coaching.   I. Title
    GV951.8.H38   1995
    796.332'2--dc20   94-18037
                                                                        CIP

ISBN: 0-87322-574-0

Photos on pages 11, 59, 107 are courtesy of *The Daily Illini*, University of Illinois. Photo on page 131 is courtesy of David Hawkes.

Developmental Editor: Julia Anderson; **Assistant Editors**: Julie Marx Ohnemus, Anna Curry, and Hank Woolsey; **Copyeditor**: John Wentworth; **Proofreader**: Kezia E. Endsley; **Text Designer, Typesetter, and Layout**: Doug Burnett; **Photo Editor**: Karen Maier; **Cover Designer**: Jack Davis; **Photographer (cover)**: © F-Stock/Brian Drake; **Illustrator**: Michael Larson; **Printer**: United Graphics

Printed in the United States of America   15   14   13   12   11

Human Kinetics
Web site: www.HumanKinetics.com

United States: Human Kinetics, P.O. Box 5076, Champaign, IL 61825-5076
800-747-4457
e-mail: humank@hkusa.com

Canada: Human Kinetics, 475 Devonshire Road, Unit 100, Windsor, ON N8Y 2L5
800-465-7301 (in Canada only)
e-mail: orders@hkcanada.com

Europe: Human Kinetics, 107 Bradford Road, Stanningley
Leeds LS28 6AT, United Kingdom
+44 (0) 113 255 5665
e-mail: hk@hkeurope.com

Australia: Human Kinetics, 57A Price Avenue, Lower Mitcham, South Australia 5062
08 8277 1555
e-mail: liahka@senet.com.au

New Zealand: Human Kinetics, P.O. Box 105-231, Auckland Central
09-523-3462
e-mail: hkp@ihug.co.nz

Contents

Foreword   v

Acknowledgments   vii

Introduction   ix

Play Finders   1

Part I Running Plays   11

    Inside Plays   14

    Off-Tackle Plays   24

    Outside Plays   45

Part II Passing Plays   59

    Play Action Passes   62

    Dropback Passes   88

Part III Special Plays   107

    Reverses   109

    Throwbacks   114

    PATs   117

    Trick Plays   120

Summary   123

Play Terminology   125

Coaches Index   127

About the Editor   131

Foreword

Football coaches seldom do or see things the same way. Our differences are especially apparent in our offensive schemes. We all have unique characteristics in the formations, types of motion, and plays that we run. We do, however, have one thing in common: A belief that the offensive system we use offers our team the greatest chance for success.

Sometimes, though, our allegiance to a certain system or formation prevents us from seeing the possible adaptations from other coaches, other systems, and other formations. And that's a shame. After all, we share the same goals—to score or maintain possession of the football.

Football's Best Offensive Playbook is a great opportunity for all of us who coach to broaden our vision, appreciate our differences, respect what other coaches have to offer, and learn what we can from the plays the book provides. Resources like this help us increase our knowledge of the game and appreciate its diversity. Plus, it's just plain fun leafing through this tremendous collection of Xs and Os.

The college and high school coaches who contributed plays to this book are among the best in our profession. The national and conference titles, number of wins, and winning percentage represented by this group is staggering. I can only imagine the number of touchdowns their teams have scored using the offensive plays described here.

Some of the plays you'll recognize. You may have run them yourself, seen them on TV, or had opponents run them against you. For example, I get to see Bobby Bowden's "46 Toss" sweep from the sideline each year when we play Florida State. Frankly, seeing it again on page 45 didn't bring back fond memories. That play is a proven winner, like all the other plays you'll find here.

This playbook allows coaches, players, and fans alike to be students of the game. My father, a retired football coach, is sure to enjoy it. My college coach, Jim Sweeney (p. 114), will certainly have a copy in his office. And I can think of several other friends and colleagues I'll recommend it to.

Dee Hawkes, a longtime coaching friend from my years in Washington, has pulled together these 102 plays and organized them into a useful format. The diagrams are clear and accurate. The descriptions are concise and insightful. What makes the book extra special are the coaches' insights and in-depth descriptions of each play. This kind of information is rarely shared outside of our clinics or team meetings, so take advantage of this opportunity to enhance your offensive system. You'll find at least a few plays to add to your own playbook. And when you use them in a game, I hope that they work—unless you're playing my team.

Dennis Erickson
Head Coach, University of Miami

Acknowledgments

My sincere thanks to the coaches who contributed their best plays for those who love the game. Anyone who has been involved in offensive football recognizes the strong influences of these outstanding college and high school coaches. They have been invaluable in explaining their plays. Without them, there would have been no book. Special thanks to Coach Dennis Erickson for writing the foreword.

I wish to thank the college SIDs and assistant coaches who contributed technical information for their head coaches. I especially thank assistant coaches Bill Diedrick (Washington), Mike Dunbar (Toledo), and Ken Flajole (Missouri) for their wise counsel.

I am deeply grateful to Michael Larson, who used his gifts as a graphic artist to skillfully draw the plays. I thank him for his patience and commitment to this book.

My thanks to the editors at Human Kinetics who very professionally shared their editorial expertise with the new kid on the block. Ted Miller opened up the publishing world to me, and I value his mentorship, candor, organizational skills, and football knowledge that helped to make the book more readable. Julia Anderson, the developmental editor, also earned my regard with the sensitivity she showed to a first-time author. Copyeditor, John Wentworth, read and critiqued my manuscript like the pro he is. Doug Burnett did a terrific job creating the interior design, especially the play format. Finally, I appreciate the enthusiasm of publicity manager Jolene Rupe, who said we were producing a "good book."

On a personal note, I want to thank my children, David and Leanne, who were always available to offer encouragement when I needed a pickup. I am indebted to Judy, my wife, for generously retyping text, listening to my concerns, and speaking out when she felt I was drifting. Without her help, writing this book would have been a lot more work and a lot less fun.

Introduction

The game of football has changed significantly since Rutgers and Princeton squared off in the first game on November 6, 1869. At that time, the rules of play were decided by the two team captains. Kicking was allowed, but there was no running or passing. Although I'm not quite old enough to recall the plays used by those two teams, during my 32 years of coaching I have seen just about every imaginable offensive play. Plays I haven't seen first-

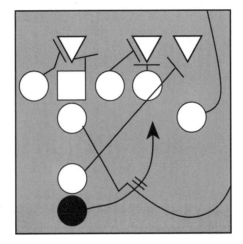

hand I've obtained through clinic notes, coaching magazines, films, books, and conversations with colleagues.

The Xs and Os of football are fascinating. With 11 offensive players symbolized by circles (or Os) and 11 defensive players represented by triangles (or Xs), the options for attack and counterattack are limited only by the width and length of the field and the strategist's imagination. Play diagrams can be impressively presented with today's high-tech video. But more often plays are scribbled onto a handy notepad or sketched on a restaurant's paper napkin by coaches like you who are capturing an inspired thought or comparing notes during a meal. Who will know the difference if next season's blocking scheme or formation was crafted between ketchup and mustard stains?

The easiest way to start a conversation with a football coach is to ask about his best play. The idea for this book, in fact, came over 20 years ago when I was drinking coffee in a Chicago hotel bar. The hotel was packed with attendees from the American Football Coaches Association (AFCA) convention. I struck up a conversation with a man sitting a stool away, an unemployed line coach stopping to see some friends on his way to a job interview in Los

Angeles. When I asked for his favorite play, he pulled out a napkin, borrowed my pen, and drew an inside trap play. Despite bar noises and interruptions, his concentration never faltered during his explanation. The coach was Chuck Knox, who became head coach of the Los Angeles Rams in 1973. His passionate description triggered the idea for this book on best plays.

All of us have our favorite offensive plays. And we all have our favorite offensive systems. These preferences lead to the distinctive style of offensive coaching that makes football so exciting.

You hold in your hands the best offensive plays of many of the most successful football coaches from across the U.S. You'll find all types of offensive formations and plays, from One-Back to Fullhouse and from play action passes to goal line power running plays. The plays come from coaches of both college and high school football. Each play includes key coaching points and insights into strategy for using the play. And although the presentation is standardized, the descriptions are in the special language of each coach.

The coaches represented here have spent years coaching and are outstanding teachers. They were selected through the recommendations of their coaching colleagues. I strived to collect the best and most diverse offensive plays from coaches in all regions of the United States, with about half of the plays from college coaches and the other half from high school coaches. It's safe to say that *Football's Best Offensive Playbook* lives up to its title.

To make it convenient for you, the book is divided into three parts: running plays, passing plays, and special plays. The running plays are divided into three sections, according to their point of attack: inside, off-tackle, and outside. The passing plays are organized into play action or dropback groupings. And the always fun special plays are categorized under reverses, throwbacks, PATs, and trick plays. Convenient play finders are provided to help you locate plays that fall into meaningful classifications.

Study this playbook next to your own. You might want to add your own wrinkle or two to a play you find here. The best coaches are always looking for a way to gain the competitive edge. It just may be that a play from this book could help your team win a crucial game. But if a play you've borrowed from this book does pay off, don't feel obligated to thank the coach who contributed it. After all, you were smart enough to use it! Good luck and many touchdowns to all of you.

Formation

Play	Play number	Coach	Page
I-Formation			
Right Stack Counter 8 Speed	1	Gerry DiNardo	14
Left Pro-ISO Right	2	Gary Gibbs	15
Ole Miss TB Trap Draw	3	Billy Brewer	16
Blast Left Bend Right	4	John McKissick	17
Power Off-Tackle	11	Roy Kidd	24
44 Power	12	Larry Thomas	25
57 Power	13	Bob Stone	26
24 Slice	14	R.C. Slocum	27
31 Scissors	15	Ronnie Haushalter	28
34	16	Tom Downing	29
Sprint Draw	17	Don Soldinger	30
25 Sprint Draw	18	John Cooper	31
*Jumbo Right 76 Read	19	Dennis Kozlowski	32
*Wedge 2nd Man	20	Dick Tighe	33
46 Toss	32	Bobby Bowden	45
58 Toss Sweep	33	Chuck Mizerski	46
41 Pitch	34	Tom Osborne	47
38 Option	35	Barry Alvarez	48
Belly Option	36	Mack Brown	49
Toss Sweep Right	37	Herb Deromedi	50
224 Z Dig	45	Keith Gilbertson	62
Right I Pro 23 Cross Boot	46	Ron Schipper	63
417 Kansas	47	Glen Mason	64
I-Right Sprint Draw 4 Pass X Option	48	Steve Spurrier	65
Crack Screen Left	49	Rick Brooks	66

* Power-I Formation

Play	Play number	Coach	Page
I-Formation			
Boot Right	50	Mike Huard	67
Cross Buck Pass	51	Tom Marcucci	68
I-Right Counter Pass Right	52	Al Fracassa	69
Trap Option Pass	53	Joe Kinnan	70
Counter 23 Pass	54	Rich Zinanni	71
Play Pass 33-37 Double Cross	55	Wally Sheets	72
Pro Set Right 77 Pass	56	Freddie James	73
470 Scan	57	Gary Moeller	74
71 B Option	71	Spike Dykes	88
49 Tailback Screen	72	Dick Dullaghan	89
Z Reverse	90	Terry Donahue	109
Right 22 Reverse at 9	91	Dexter Wood	110
Belly 58 Reverse	92	Bob Deter	111
Z Reverse Throwback to QB	95	Jim Sweeney	114
One-Back			
Spread Left 31 Trap	9	Tom Moore	22
34 Zone	23	Sonny Lubick	36
35 Zone	24	Chuck Tarbox	37
Toss 48	38	Bill Lewis	51
96	62	Jimmie Keeling	79
Pro Right 32 Naked	63	Jim Wacker	80
Ace Right Jet Strong Z F	64	Joe Petricca	81
Left 5 Naked Pitch	65	Dave Roberts	82
Slot Shovel Right	66	Lou Tepper	83
Doubles Left 71 X	73	Dennis Erickson	90
Doubles Right 168 Shallow/Wide	74	Jim Donnan	91
82 Up	75	Tom Grippa	92
40 Y/A Option	76	Jerry Schliem	93
Dubs Right 93X-Divide	77	Jack Stark	94
Spread Right Rip 60 Go	78	Alan Paturzo	95

Play	Play number	Coach	Page
Left Cat Bunch 247 Pivot	79	Steve Axman	96
316 Double Reverse Pass	94	Mike Price	113
Split Backs			
16 Handback	10	John Harvill	23
42 Counter Trap	25	Eric Roanhaus	38
Split Right Switch Motion Left 56	26	Gil Rector	39
528	67	Terry Allen	84
49 Rail	68	Joe Miller	85
Flackin Right	69	Frosty Westering	86
Red Right 86 X Post	80	John Mackovic	97
Split Right 958	81	LaVell Edwards	98
74-75 Double Seam	82	Tom Coughlin	99
52 Stop	83	Jim Caldwell	100
Brown 538 Angle	84	Bruce Snyder	101
Check Pass	85	Jack Johnson	102
Z Burst	86	Harry Welch	103
Cowboy Under Left	97	Jim Ragland	116
Wing-T			
Wing Right Tackle Trap Short	5	Jerry Horowitz	18
White Quick 34 Trap Zip	6	Terry Ennis	19
Halfback at 0	7	Bob Giannunzio	20
46 Counter	8	Bob Reade	21
35 Draw	21	Tam Hollingshead	34
983 XBL	22	Art Fiore	35
58 Pass 911 X	59	Tony Severino	76
20 Waggle	60	Jim Sauls	77
48 Pass	61	Walt Braun	78
26 Reverse	93	Max Hawk	112
121 Waggle Throwback	96	Brian O'Reilly	115

Play	Play number	Coach	Page
Bone			
T36 Power	28	John Jenkins	41
Red 34 Belly	29	Alan Chadwick	42
Inside Read Option	41	Ken Hatfield	51
344 Crazy	98	Pete Levine	117
Woody One	99	Mac Barousse	118
Special Left Pull	100	Bruce Reynolds	119
Trips			
89 Sally at 3	31	Harold Raymond	44
Trips Right–Belly Option Right	43	Herb Meyer	56
Trey Left Fan Right 94 Y Choice	87	Bob McQueen	104
Z Statue Left	102	Bennie Edens	121
Double Slot			
Spread 12	42	Bob Wagner	55
956 Waggle Pass	58	Jim Nagel	75
20 Read	88	Don Read	105
Gangster Pass Right: Curl & Out	89	Jeff Scurran	106
Fullhouse			
T36	30	Timothy Jaureguito	43
Pro			
80 X-Out	70	Bill Mallory	87
Flea Flicker Left	101	Nick Hyder	120
Double Wing			
Wingback Trap Option	44	Jarrell Williams	57
Veer			
46 Veer	27	Rocky Hager	40
29 Option	39	Jim Walden	52
28 Option	40	Bruce Keith	53

Running Plays

Play	Play number	Page
Power		
Left Pro-ISO Right	2	15
Power Off-Tackle	11	24
44 Power	12	25
57 Power	13	26
24 Slice	14	27
Jumbo Right 76 Read	19	32
Wedge 2nd Man	20	33
983 XBL	22	35
Split Right Switch Motion Left 56	26	39
T36 Power	28	41
Red 34 Belly	29	42
T36	30	43
Speed		
Right Stack Counter 8 Speed	1	14
White Quick 34 Trap Zip	6	19
34	16	29
35 Zone	24	37
46 Veer	27	40
46 Toss	32	45
58 Toss Sweep	33	46
41 Pitch	34	47
38 Option	35	48
Toss Sweep Right	37	50
Toss 48	38	51
28 Option	40	53
Deception		
Ole Miss TB Trap Draw	3	16
Blast Left Bend Right	4	17
Wing Right Tackle Trap Short	5	18
Halfback at 0	7	20
46 Counter	8	21

Play	Play number	Page
Spread Left 31 Trap	9	22
16 Handback	10	23
Sprint Draw	17	30
25 Sprint Draw	18	31
35 Draw	21	34
42 Counter Trap	25	38
89 Sally at 3	31	44
Belly Option	36	49
29 Option	39	52
Trips Right-Belly Option Right	43	56
Z Reverse	90	109
Right 22 Reverse at 9	91	110
Belly 58 Reverse	92	111
Z Statue Left	102	121

Traps

Ole Miss TB Trap Draw	3	16
Wing Right Tackle Trap Short	5	18
White Quick 34 Trap Zip	6	19
46 Counter	8	21
Spread Left 31 Trap	9	22
42 Counter Trap	25	38
Wingback Trap Option	44	57

Draws

Ole Miss TB Trap Draw	3	16
Sprint Draw	17	30
25 Sprint Draw	18	31
35 Draw	21	34

Option

Right Stack Counter 8 Speed	1	14
38 Option	35	48
Belly Option	36	49
29 Option	39	52

Play	Play number	Page
28 Option	40	53
Inside Read Option	41	54
Trips Right-Belly Option Right	43	56
Wingback Trap Option	44	57
Sweep		
35 Zone	24	37
46 Toss	32	45
58 Toss Sweep	33	46
41 Pitch	34	47
Toss Sweep Right	37	50
Toss 48	38	51
Short Yardage		
Left Pro-ISO Right	2	15
Power Off-Tackle	11	24
44 Power	12	25
57 Power	13	26
Jumbo Right 76 Read	19	32
Wedge 2nd Man	20	33
T36 Power	28	41
Red 34 Belly	29	42
T36	30	43
Long Yardage		
46 Veer	27	40
89 Sally at 3	31	44
46 Toss	32	45
58 Toss Sweep	33	46
41 Pitch	34	47
Toss Sweep Right	37	50
29 Option	39	52
28 Option	40	53

Passing Plays

Play	Play number	Page
Screens		
Crack Screen Left	49	66
49 Tailback Screen	72	89
Shovel		
96	62	79
Left 5 Naked Pitch	65	82
Slot Shovel Right	66	83
Bootleg		
Right I Pro 23 Cross Boot	46	63
Boot Right	50	67
Counter 23 Pass	54	71
956 Waggle Pass	58	75
58 Pass 911 X	59	76
20 Waggle	60	77
48 Pass	61	78
Pro Right 32 Naked	63	80
Short Yardage		
I-Right Counter Pass Right	52	69
Flackin Right	69	86
80 X-Out	70	87
71 B Option	71	88
49 Tailback Screen	72	89
Split Right 958	81	98
Brown 538 Angle	84	101
Check Pass	85	102
Gangster Pass Right: Curl & Out	89	106
Special Left Pull	100	119

Play	Play number	Page
Long Yardage		
224 Z Dig	45	62
417 Kansas	47	64
I-Right Sprint Draw 4 Pass X Option	48	65
Cross Buck Pass	51	68
Counter 23 Pass	54	71
Play Pass 33-37 Double Cross	55	72
Pro Set Right 77 Pass	56	73
470 Scan	57	74
82 Up	75	92
Left Cat Bunch 247 Pivot	79	96
Red Right 86 X Post	80	97
74-75 Double Seam	82	99
52 Stop	83	100
Check Pass	85	102
316 Double Reverse Pass	94	113

Key to Play Diagrams

Symbol	Meaning	Symbol	Meaning
○	Offensive player	N	Noseguard
□	Center	T	Defensive tackle
TE	Tight end	E	Defensive end
SE	Split end	OB	Outside linebacker
FL	Flanker (outside receiver on side of tight end)	LB	Inside linebacker
WR	Wide receiver (split end or flanker)	CB	Cornerback
X	Single receiver (usually split side)	SS	Strong safety
Y	Tight end (inside receiver on side of Z)	FS	Free safety
Z	Flanker (outside receiver on side of Y)	⊤	Blocking
TB	Tailback	⋁⋀⋁	Man in motion
FB	Fullback	⫾	Pulling lineman
HB	Halfback	→	Path of player (Off.)
WB	Wingback	●	Ball carrier
SB	Slotback	◐	May handle the ball
RB	Running back	─┼┼─	Handoff
A	A back	─ ─ ─	Passed ball
B	B back	●──	Pass release spot
C	C back	→	Path of player (Def.)
H	H back		

Part I

Running Plays

The days of the flying wedge and the three-yards-and-a-cloud-of-dust philosophy are long gone. Conservative coaches who taught only a smash-mouth, straight ahead running game have been replaced by offensive coordinators who devise diverse offensive sets, employ a variety of motion, and throw as often as they run on first down. And yet the running game is still the basis of a successful offensive attack.

I'm pleased to include plays from coaches who have established their teams as perennial national contenders through the running game. Great coaches like Tom Osborne at Nebraska, Bob Reade at Augustana (IL), and John McKissick of Summerville High School (SC) contributed their most successful plays—the ones that opposing defensive coordinators spend countless hours and sleepless nights trying, futilely, to devise schemes to stop. Perhaps after reading the coaches' strategic secrets for using these plays, their opponents will have more success. But don't count on it.

The collection of plays in this part attest to the multidimensional running game used in college and high school football. The I and Wing-T formations are preferred, but most of the plays can be run from a number of sets. For running off-tackle and between the tackles you'll find the usual favorites: traps, power plays, counters, and draws. And for getting outside, the top choices are the toss

and the option pitch or handoff.

The same trends in the running game that you see on Friday nights or Saturday afternoons are reflected in the plays provided here. To take advantage of today's fast and versatile backs, plays that allow the runner to pick his hole, cut back, or outrun the defense are in style. One of the best things happening in the running game is the popularity of the option. Common too are plays that allow the all-purpose quarterback to hand off the ball or tuck it under his own arm and run with it. A straight dropback quarterback would have problems executing many of the plays on the list.

Some of the plays may look and sound the same, but check out the blocking schemes— they're different. And so are the coaches' strategies for using the plays. As you know, very few coaches think exactly alike. You'll have fun, as I did, as you compare and contrast the coaches' when-and-why reasoning.

If you don't find a few good new running plays—or some new wrinkles for plays you're already using—then either you haven't really tried or you're a genius (and you'll be in my next book). And if I see that your team is running the ball much better next season, I'll know that you did try, and that you did what every coaching genius does—steal ideas from the coaches whose teams run the ball the best.

Play List

Coach	Play	Formation
Inside Plays		
Gerry DiNardo	Right Stack Counter 8 Speed	I
Gary Gibbs	Left Pro-ISO Right	I
Billy Brewer	Ole Miss TB Trap Draw	I
John McKissick	Blast Left Bend Right	I
Jerry Horowitz	Wing Right Tackle Trap Short	Wing-T
Terry Ennis	White Quick 34 Trap Zip	Wing-T
Bob Giannunzio	Halfback at 0	Wing-T
Bob Reade	46 Counter	Wing-T
Tom Moore	Spread Left 31 Trap	One-Back
John Harvill	16 Handback	Split Backs
Off-Tackle Plays		
Roy Kidd	Power Off-Tackle	I
Larry Thomas	44 Power	I
Bob Stone	57 Power	I
R.C. Slocum	24 Slice	I
Ronnie Haushalter	31 Scissors	I
Tom Downing	34	I
Don Soldinger	Sprint Draw	I
John Cooper	25 Sprint Draw	I
Dennis Kozlowski	Jumbo Right 76 Read	Power-I
Dick Tighe	Wedge 2nd Man	Power-I
Tam Hollingshead	35 Draw	Wing-T
Art Fiore	983 XBL	Wing-T
Sonny Lubick	34 Zone	One-Back
Chuck Tarbox	35 Zone	One-Back
Eric Roanhaus	42 Counter Trap	Split Backs
Gil Rector	Split Right Switch Motion Left 56	Split Backs
Rocky Hager	46 Veer	Veer

Coach	Play	Formation
John Jenkins	T36 Power	Bone
Alan Chadwick	Red 34 Belly	Bone
Timothy Jaureguito	T36	Fullhouse
Harold Raymond	89 Sally At 3	Trips
Outside Plays		
Bobby Bowden	46 Toss	I
Chuck Mizerski	58 Toss Sweep	I
Tom Osborne	41 Pitch	I
Barry Alvarez	38 Option	I
Mack Brown	Belly Option	I
Herb Deromedi	Toss Sweep Right	I
Bill Lewis	Toss 48	One-Back
Jim Walden	29 Option	Veer
Bruce Keith	28 Option	Veer
Ken Hatfield	Inside Read Option	Bone
Bob Wagner	Spread 12	Double Slot
Herb Meyer	Trips Right–Belly Option Right	Trips
Jarrell Williams	Wingback Trap Option	Double Wing

Gerry DiNardo

Vanderbilt University

Nashville, Tennessee

Southeastern
Conference (1-A)

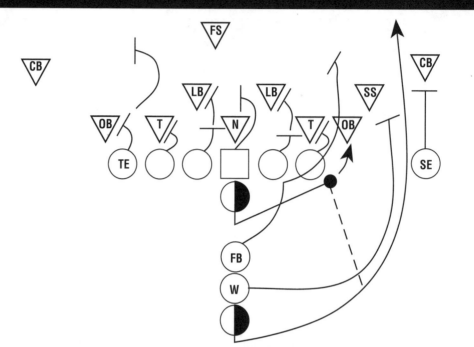

Right Stack Counter 8 Speed

Play Strategy	Player Assignments	Coaching Points

Play Strategy

By design, the Counter 8 Speed is a TB sweep that can be run on any down. The QB can audible to the play. Eight out of 10 times the ball is pitched. When the secondary is blocked, the Counter 8 Speed has big-play potential.

Player Assignments

Formation: **I-Formation**

Offensive Linemen

RT: Zone blocks with RG vs. 41, 4, or 5

RG: Gets call from RT, zone blocks with RT vs. 41, 4, or 5. Based on call, power or outside base blocks vs. 21, 2, or 3.

C: Combo blocks Nose with LG.

LG: Combo blocks Nose with C.

LT: Base cut blocks man on.

Receivers and Backs

SE: Blocks deep 1/3 coverage.

TE: Runs through for backside CB.

FB: Zone schemes with RG and RT, releases upfield, and blocks FS.

W: Runs playside, circles the defender, and blocks inside containment.

TB: Freeze steps with QB, stays in pitch phase, and looks to receive the pitch.

QB: Locates EMOL for pitch key, freezes action for 2 steps, and attacks pitch key.

Coaching Points

■ Reading the pitch key correctly is essential to the play's success. First, the RT checks the pitch key and blocks the next defender inside. If uncovered, the RT reach blocks or power blocks based on pitch key location.

■ If the DT is playing heavy on veer responsibility, reach blocking is made easier for the RT. Secondary blocking support comes from ARC block by W on containment. The FB runs past zone to block FS. The SE maintains contact with CB; TE keeps the backside CB from crossing the field.

■ The QB attacks the pitch key downhill to run in the crease or pitch to the TB.

■ The TB alerts the "hot" call to the QB.

Left Pro-ISO Right

2

Gary Gibbs

University of Oklahoma

Norman, Oklahoma

Big Eight Conference
(1A)

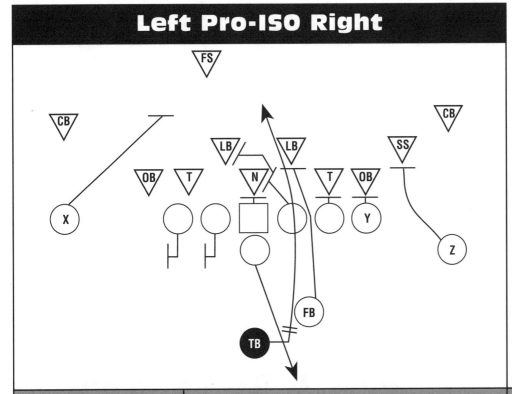

Play Strategy	Player Assignments	Coaching Points

Play Strategy

The beauty of this basic play is that it can be called any time. Coaches prefer it against the 50 defense because of the ability to get a clean block on the LB. It is a good early down call. It is always run to the TE side from the I-oriented two-back set. Depending on the tempo of the game, defenses can be caught off guard on long-yardage situations. This play action pass can be called after ISO has been established and the defense is expecting a run.

Player Assignments

Formation: **I-Formation**

Offensive Lineman

FST: If covered, solo sets to reach man or to take him wherever he goes. If uncovered, sets to block LB over.

FSG: If covered, solo sets to reach man on him. If uncovered, power sets; pinches Nose.

C: If covered, sets Nose; guard pinches.

BSG: If covered, power sets. C helps. If uncovered, short fan blocks #1 on LOS.

BST: Short fan blocks #2 on LOS.

Receivers and Backs

Y: If covered, sets up to pass block #3.

X: Releases inside; blocks FS.

Z: Releases inside; blocks SS.

FB: First blocks LB middle to inside.

TB: Aims at inside leg of guard.

QB: Fronts out, runs straight back, and hands off to TB deep.

Coaching Points

■ The main emphasis of this inside running play is to get upfield until past the LBs. At that time the back reads whether to break.

■ The QB appears to be going back to pass but instead hands off and sets up for a pass. It is vital that the QB's technique be the same on this play as on its companion play, the ISO Pass.

■ It is a must for the FB to have a clean block against a 50 defense.

■ Can run ISO out of any 1 oriented 2 back set, but it must run to TE side.

3

Billy Brewer

University of Mississippi

Oxford, Mississippi

(1983–93)

Southeastern Conference (1A)

Ole Miss TB Trap Draw

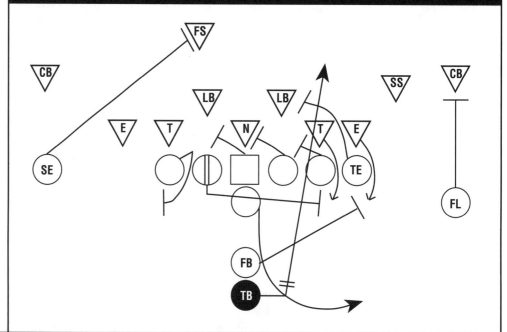

Play Strategy	Player Assignments	Coaching Points

Play Strategy

The dean of the SEC coaches runs his TB Trap Draw play during any short-yardage situations. It is effective against pressure defenses. Coach Brewer has no hesitation calling this off-tackle play anywhere, which includes coming out from his goal line or attacking in the red zone.

Player Assignments

Formation: **I-Formation**

Offensive Linemen

PST: If guard is covered, combo blocks DL to first LB inside. If guard is uncovered, blocks first LB inside.

PSG: If covered, combo blocks DL to first LB inside. If uncovered, combo blocks Nose to offside LB.

C: If covered, combo blocks Nose to offside LB. If uncovered, blocks back for pulling guard.

BSG: Traps the first DL past the PST; vs. 40 with deuce call, seals the LB.

BST: Seals the B gap to wide rush.

Receivers and Backs

FL: Releases downfield; blocks CB.

TE: If tackle is covered, blocks first LB inside. If tackle is uncovered, blocks #4 (SS).

SE: Sprints hard to block FS.

FB: Load blocks on #3 (DE)

TB: Uses landmark on the inside hip of the PST; receives handoff from QB.

QB: Fronts out and between second and third step hands off to TB.

Coaching Points

■ The trap draw eliminates one-on-one line blocking.

■ The pulling guard (LG) is coached to pick up the LB, not the DT, when the deuce call is made.

■ The strength of the blocking schemes gives all linemen blocking angles and leverage.

■ TB allows pulling guard to get past PSG; TB coached to not be too fast.

Blast Left Bend Right

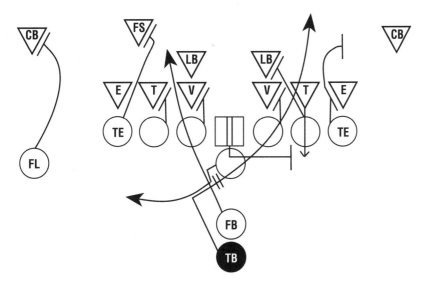

John McKissick

Summerville High School

Summerville, South Carolina

Play Strategy	Player Assignments	Coaching Points

Play Strategy

Coach McKissick runs his Blast Bend play after successfully using the blast play several times. Play selection depends on what the defense is doing to stop the inside blast play. The weaponry plays, which also include the quick pitch and isolation plays, are run from double tight to obtain maximum blocking at the POA.

Player Assignments

Formation: **I-Formation**

Offensive Linemen

RT: Releases inside; blocks inside LB.

RG: If covered, blocks man on. If uncovered, blocks out on DT.

C: If covered, blocks Nose. If uncovered, pulls playside and trap blocks DT.

LG: If covered, blocks man on. If uncovered, blocks Nose with C.

LT: Blocks man on or outside.

Receivers and Backs

FL: Releases downfield; blocks CB.

RE: Releases to block CB; vs. even defense, holds up DE first.

LE: Releases to block FS; vs. odd defense, holds up DE first.

FB: Aims inside leg of LG, fakes handoff, and blocks LB.

TB: Follows FB, runs cutback, and receives handoff.

QB: Reverse pivots, fakes handoff to FB, hands back to TB, and runs backside.

Coaching Points

- If the DEs are coming hard, the TE on that side must delay the rush.

- Versus even, the C pulls playside to block DT. C must be alert for the slant tackle.

- The QB has the option to call the blast play anytime he wants.

- Both guards are split 2 feet. This is essential on weaponry plays like the Blast Bend.

5

Jerry Horowitz

John F. Kennedy High School

Bronx, New York

Wing Right Tackle Trap Short

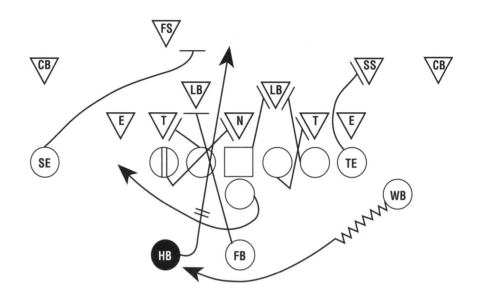

Play Strategy

Coach Horowitz's unique Wing-T play fits well as a misdirection play in the belly series. The play can be run from any formation where there is a FB and HB. It fits nicely into any down situation. The HB's path stays the same vs. even or split defenses, although the blocking schemes may change. A good draw play if WB motion is away from formation. Also used as a misdirect play in the belly series.

Player Assignments

Formation: **Wing-T**

Offensive Linemen

PST: Blocks first inside LB.

PSG: Sets up, shows pass, and blocks out on DT.

C: Is responsible for area through playside; blocks first LB.

BSG: Blocks out on DT.

BST: Pulls, trap blocks first defender past BSG.

Receivers and Backs

PSE: Influences blocks inside; goes upfield to block SS.

BSE: Blocks the middle 1/3.

WB: Runs motion; options to run in front or behind set backs.

FB: Blocks the backside LB.

TB: Rock steps, aims for PSG's far foot, and receives handoff from QB.

QB: Reverses out at 140 degrees past midline, keeps the ball tucked, and seats ball on TB's belly fake option.

Coaching Points

■ If the Nose rides the C, he works upfield toward the second level.

■ The BSG must not hesitate while blocking out on the DT.

■ Coming from behind, fly motion gives the WB an opportunity to run the fake option.

■ The FB must avoid both the pulling BST and the QB, who is stepping toward the HB.

■ The HB is coached to rock step, not step away. He continues straight upfield or bounces outside when in open field.

■ The play is designed to be run against an odd defense. The rationale for this is that few defenses teach the Nose to play the trap block.

White Quick 34 Trap Zip

6

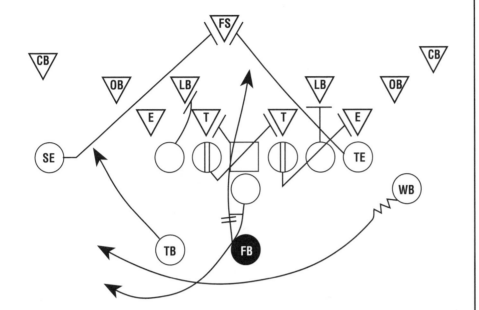

Terry Ennis

Cascade High School
Everett, Washington

Play Strategy	Player Assignments	Coaching Points

Play Strategy

The 34 Trap can be run in any situation. It has been very successful on third and long. The inside trap is used in conjunction with the sweep and the bootleg, which utilizes the same cross-back movement. Coach Ennis likes to run the play against inside LBs who are aligned deep or who flow fast. Another reason for calling the trap is to prevent the DT from penetrating into the backfield. This play can be run from any formation that has the FB directly behind the C.

Player Assignments

Formation: **Wing-T**

Offensive Linemen

OFT: Releases flat inside; blocks first LB on the off-side.

OFG: Pulls; traps first man past the C on the LOS.

C: Versus odd, double team blocks the Nose; vs. even, fills for OFG.

ONG: Versus odd, double team blocks the Nose; vs. even, runs influence block.

ONT: Releases flat inside; blocks the first LB inside.

Receivers and Backs

TE: Blocks first LB outside the ONT. Releases inside flat, hard 8 yards deep; blocks FS.

SE: Releases flat, hard 8 yards deep off center; blocks FS.

WB: Releases to downfield; blocks SS.

TB: Fakes a 21 sweep.

FB: Receives handoff from QB, explodes into the POA.

QB: Opens with back to the POA, hands off to FB, makes sweep fake, and runs bootleg.

Coaching Points

■ Strong downfield middle blocking is provided by the SE and TE.

■ The WB can run a short "zip" motion to give the defense another adjustment.

■ QB may run the play with a "check-with-me" call at the LOS. While handing the ball off to the FB, the QB jab steps with his onside foot, opens with his back to the POA, and points his foot to the opposite goal line. The sweep fake and bootleg action must keep the defense guessing.

■ The FB steps with his onside foot to the midline of the QB. His second step is straight ahead, which creates a tight mesh with the QB. Upon receiving the ball, the FB plants his outside foot and angles to the POA, reading the defensive front. Versus the odd, he hugs the double team and veers off of it. Versus the even, he runs more straight-ahead and looks to pick up downfield blocks by the ends.

7

Bob Giannunzio

Norway High School

Norway, Michigan

Halfback at 0

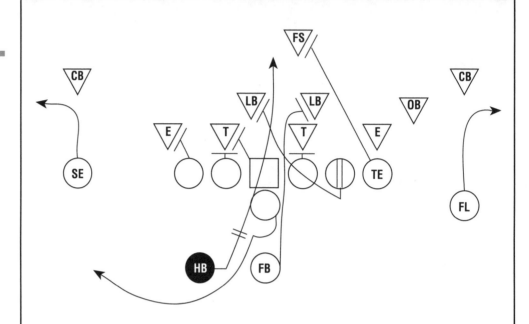

Play Strategy	Player Assignments	Coaching Points
Coach Giannunzio calls this inside play on any down when short yardage is needed. The play is set up by running the FB as a diveback at the 2 hole. Another option has the QB faking to both backs and running a naked bootleg to the playside corner.	Formation: **Wing-T** **Offensive Lineman** **RT:** Runs loop block behind the RG; blocks weakside LB. **RG:** Blocks out on defender over or outside gap. **C:** Double-team blocks man over LG. **LG:** Double-team blocks man on with C. **LT:** Seals off the DE. **Receivers and Backs** **RE:** Releases inside to block FS. **SE:** Runs an out route; seals the CB. **FL:** Runs an out route; seals the CB. **FB:** Fakes dive; runs through 2 hole. **HB:** Steps right, runs dive through 1 hole, and takes ball from QB. **QB:** Reverse pivots, fakes to FB with open hand, gives ball to HB, gets depth, and runs to the playside corner.	▪ After making a good fake, the FB collides with or blocks the LB. ▪ The horizontal stretch of the two wide receivers helps spread the secondary away from the middle. ▪ The HB hugs the double-team block and cuts off the RT's block of the weakside LB. ▪ By releasing inside, the RE prevents the DE from closing too fast. ▪ Versus the 44 defense, the key block comes from the RT, who pulls behind the RG. He is the lead blocker at the POA.

46 Counter

Bob Reade

Augustana College

Rock Island, Illinois

College Conference of Illinois and Wisconsin (NCAA III)

Play Strategy	Player Assignments	Coaching Points

Play Strategy

Coach Reade likes this play because it provides the opportunity to hit quickly with inside power away from the flow. He calls this misdirection play in any situation where the inside LBs are flowing fast and need to be slowed down. The play looks very similar to the off-tackle option.

Player Assignments

Formation: **Wing-T**

Offensive Linemen

RT: Pulls and traps first man past center.

RG: Blocks near LB.

C: Double teams the Nose with LG.

LG: Double teams the Nose with C.

LT: Releases inside to block near LB.

Receivers and Backs

SE: Drives hard to block FS.

LE: Releases inside to block SS.

FB: Runs a hard drive to inside leg of RT.

TB: Flows to right side as if to run off-tackle.

SB: Sprints hard across formation; receives inside handoff from QB; cuts up hole; runs close to double team.

QB: Reverses pivot and runs toward WB; hands off inside to WB.

Coaching Points

■ Timing is key to the success of this misdirection play.

■ The key to execution is having all four backs in a vertical line at the same time. Along that vertical line, the FB's block on the DT, the WB's acceptance of the handoff, the QB's move upfield, and the TB's fake should all occur at the same time.

■ There is no faking. Speed is the trademark of this fast hitting counter play.

9

Tom Moore

Prosser High School

Prosser, Washington

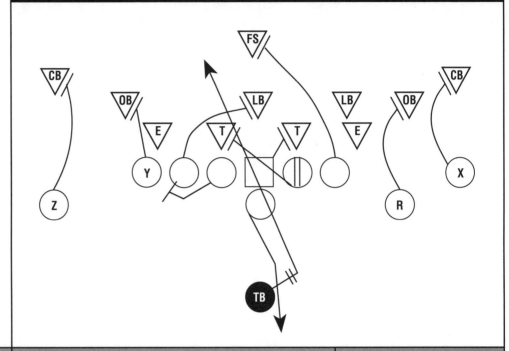

Spread Left 31 Trap

Play Strategy	Player Assignments	Coaching Points

Play Strategy

Coach Moore calls this play frequently in clutch situations. This is a favorite call on second and long when the team is in the middle of the field. To combat a no-huddle offense, the defense remains in a balanced 40 set. Play success depends on the defense having 3 in the box, with the weakside OB walked off to the open side.

Player Assignments

Formation: **One-Back**

Offensive Linemen

ST: Releases inside to block down on middle LB.

SG: Influence blocks DE.

C: Blocks backside Nose.

WG: Pulls playside to trap DT.

WT: Screens DE; runs downfield to block FS.

Receivers and Backs

Y: Runs an arc release; seals off OB.

X: Releases inside to seal off CB.

Z: Releases inside to seal off CB.

R: Releases inside to seal off OB. If not, runs downfield to block FS.

TB: Steps weakside to show pass protection. Takes handoff and follows WG trap block.

QB: Executes 3-step drop; hands off to TB on second step.

Coaching Points

■ The QB and TB timing is critical. Using a spread formation, it looks like a pass play to the defense.

■ Both wide receivers are coached to stay inside and seal off the CBs. They wait for the CBs to come.

■ The blocking scheme is designed to keep the defensive pursuit away from the middle.

16 Handback

10

John Harvill

Gaithersburg High School

Gaithersburg, Maryland

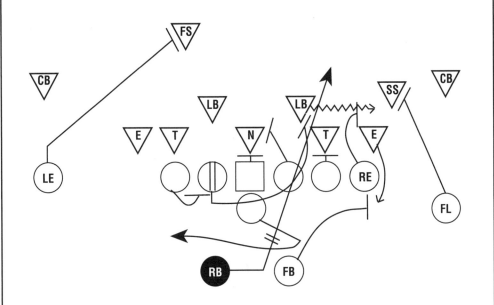

Play Strategy	Player Assignments	Coaching Points

Play Strategy

This is a very good misdirectional play from the veer offense because it hits so quickly back inside. Given these circumstances, Coach Harvill may call the play regardless of down and distance. This is his favorite misdirect play from the split-back veer.

Player Assignments

Formation: **Split Backs**

Offensive Linemen

RT: Post blocks 4 technique or 5 technique DT.

RG: Lead blocks 0 or doo-dad blocks.

C: Post blocks 0 or doo-dad blocks.

LG: Pulls playside; blocks through 2 area.

LT: Scoop blocks.

Receivers and Backs

LE: Downfield blocks FS.

RE: Lead blocks on 5 technique DT; blocks out on onside LB.

FL: Downfield blocks SS.

FB: Runs outside veer; load blocks on DE.

RB: Steps right, left, cuts on third step, takes handoff from QB, and follows the block of the pulling LG.

QB: Steps right, left, turns on third step, hands ball off to RB, and fakes bootleg left.

Coaching Points

- Versus an odd front, the Nose can be blocked by a double team or doo-dad blocking technique between C and RG.

- The pulling LG blocks through the 2 area so the RH follows into the area to read the LG's block.

- There is a good chance that both LBs may overrun the ball in reacting to the outside veer fake.

- If the LE and FL can make contact with the safeties, the play has long-yardage potential.

- First, the QB makes the play look like the Outside Veer and then hands back to the RB.

- The play is called when the defense reacts quickly to backfield flow, especially LB movement.

Roy Kidd

Eastern Kentucky University

Richmond, Kentucky

Ohio Valley Conference (1AA)

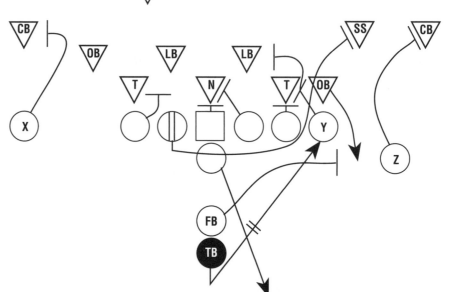

Power Off-Tackle

Play Strategy	Player Assignments	Coaching Points

Play Strategy

Although this play can be run in all situations, it is most often used in short-yardage situations. Everyone knows that the play is coming, but few teams have been able to shut it down. The TB average is over 6 yards per carry. It is the bread and butter play of the Pro-I attack.

Player Assignments

Formation: **I-Formation**

Offensive Linemen

PST: On inside: vs. 50 double team, chips with Y; vs. 4-3 double team, chips with PSG.

PSG: On inside: vs. 50 double team, chips with C; vs. 4-3 double team, chips with PST.

C: Backside on: if BSG is covered, blocks back. If BSG is uncovered, double-team chips with FSG.

BSG: Pulls to lead up through hole, looks for FS or LB.

BST: Seals inside gap.

Receivers and Backs

Y: Drives hard inside. Versus 50 double team, chips with PST. Versus 4-3 double team, looks for MLB.

X: Cuts off secondary support playside.

Z: If possible, cuts off secondary support playside. If not, blocks playside corner.

FB: Lead steps to outside hip of PST; blocks inside out on first man outside of PST block.

TB: Drops, steps with opposite foot from playside, and follows FB.

QB: Opens playside to 6 o'clock, hands to TB as deep as possible, and fakes pass.

Coaching Points

■ The depths of the TB (6-1/2 yards) and FB (4 yards) are important for proper alignment.

■ The basic line splits are 2 feet between center and guards and 3 feet between guards, tackles, and the TE. This helps in blocking the off-tackle hole.

■ The PSG listens for a cover call in case of back-side reduction along the defensive front.

■ If the BSG finds the LB running through while pulling, he kick blocks him out.

■ Versus 7 technique, the Y end releases out for support.

■ A key TB coaching point is to cram the off-tackle hole to backside, but he must not bounce outside.

44 Power

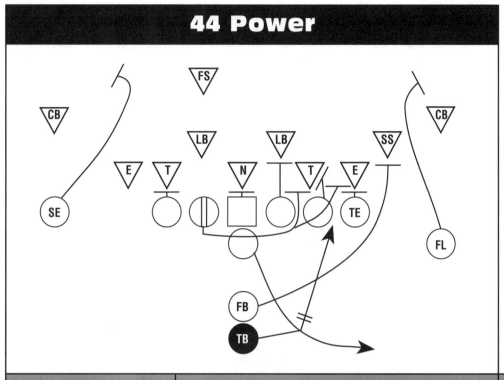

Larry Thomas

Baker High School

Baker, Louisiana

Play Strategy

Coach Thomas's most consistent play, the 44 Power is run in any situation anywhere on the field. Running at the TE side provides more blockers at the POA. If pursuit stops the TB off-tackle, he may cut back. Another alternative is for the QB to keep the ball. 43 Power is the same play run to the left.

Player Assignments

Formation: **I-Formation**

Offensive Linemen

PST: If covered, blocks man on; if uncovered, blocks inside LB.

PSG: If covered, blocks man on; if uncovered, blocks near LB.

C: If covered, blocks Nose; if uncovered, blocks backside for pulling guard.

BSG: Pulls playside; vs. odd reads block of PST as lead blocker for TB; vs. even, reads block of PSG as lead blocker for TB.

BST: Base blocks man on or outside.

Receivers and Backs

SE: Releases inside to block CB.

TE: Base blocks man on or outside.

FL: Releases inside to block CB.

FB: Runs playside to block first defender to show outside EMOL.

TB: Slides playside, receives handoff from QB, and reads the lead block of the pulling BSG.

QB: Opens playside, gains depth, hands off deep to TB, and continues to run playside.

Coaching Points

■ This off-tackle play requires the linemen to sustain their blocks as long as possible.

■ The timing between the pulling BSG and TB is essential to the success of the play.

■ The TB gets the ball deep, which allows him to read the blocking at the POA. The hole may open up inside or outside.

■ In another option, the QB fakes the handoff, turns the corner, and follows the FB's block.

13

Bob Stone

Joliet Catholic Academy

Joliet, Illinois

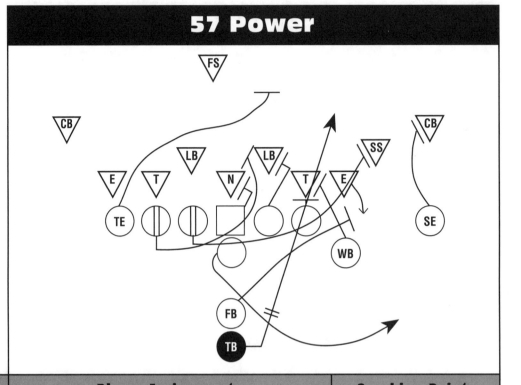

57 Power

Play Strategy

The 57 Power is used by Coach Stone in short-yardage situations to pick up a first down. A favorite tactic is to run the play on first down. The play can be run from an unbalanced Power-I set against an 8-man front.

Player Assignments

Formation: I-Formation

Offensive Linemen

ONT: Blocks #2; gets help from the WB.

ONG: Blocks #1, on or over.

C: If covered, blocks 0; if uncovered, blocks playside gap to second level.

OFG: Pulls playside to the double team. If FB kicks out DE, pulls up inside. If the FB hooks the DE, runs outside.

OFT: Blocks #1 backside or exchanges with C.

Receivers and Backs

SE: Releases downfield; blocks outside 1/3 or most dangerous defender to POA.

TE: Releases inside; blocks middle 1/3 or the FS.

WB: Blocks #2 with ONT; if possible, chips to second level.

FB: Blocks #3 on end of LOS; uses kickout block or log block.

TB: Turns, takes 2 lateral steps, plants, and receives handoff.

QB: Reverse pivots deep and wide, hands off to TB, and rolls out playside.

Coaching Points

■ The pulling guard reads the FB's block. He decides whether to run around the double team and lead the TB or run around the log block and lead the TB outside.

■ The handoff must be deep so that the TB can read and follow the block of the pulling guard.

■ The play is more successful if the WB and C can execute blocks on the second level.

24 Slice

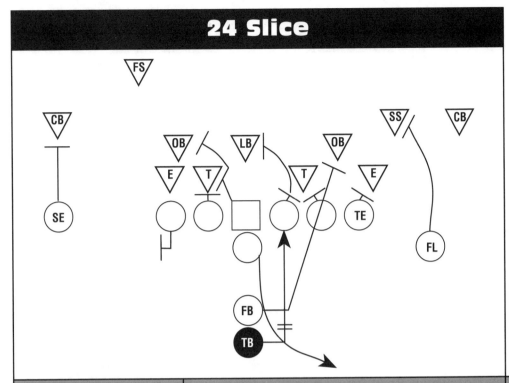

R.C. Slocum

Texas A & M University

College Station, Texas

Southwest Conference
(1A)

Play Strategy

This lead draw play to the TB is the top running play in Coach Slocum's offense. The play is effective against teams that play aggressive defense. It's not unusual to see the 24 Slice run on first or second down. The play is used in the game plan each week to adjust the blocking scheme against all 7- or 8-man fronts. The play is called when there is a separation from the upfield rush of DL and when LBs freeze or drop back into pass coverage. Getting the ball to the TB deep allows him to make a number of cuts based on the creases in the defensive front.

Player Assignments

Formation: **I-Formation**

Offensive Linemen

FST: Versus 50 (covered), single blocks man on. Stays square. Versus 40 (uncovered), double 3 technique with guard to middle LB.

FSG: Versus 50 (uncovered), double nose with center to weak inside LB. Versus 40 (covered), double 3 technique with FST.

C: Versus 50 (covered), double nose with FSG. Versus 40 (uncovered), checks backside A gap to backside LB; is responsible for backside A gap.

BSG: Versus 50 (uncovered), sets pass. Versus 40 (covered), sets quickly and blocks backside B gap.

BST: Versus 50, sets pass. He must not get beat inside. Versus 40, sets pass; is responsible for C gap.

Receivers and Backs

SE: Blocks CB.

TE: Base blocks #3. Reaches or influences.

FL: Blocks force containment.

FB: Aligns at 5 yards; shuffles. Avoids rush and blocks first inside LB to playside.

TB: Aligns at 8 yards. Pauses, shuffles, stays square to LOS, receives handoff, reads scheme, and runs to daylight.

QB: Opens at 6 o'clock; hands ball deep to TB.

Coaching Points

■ 24 Slice is a lead draw play that invites upfield rush, especially on the backside, where separation between LBs and the DL is encouraged.

■ Linemen must not let the DL retrace their steps.

■ The TE must be aggressive on #3. He must not get his hips into the hole. The FST is aggressive at the POA.

■ The FL motion can be used to get leverage to attack force DB. It is best vs. bear defense.

■ Along with the I-Formation, this play can be run from the twins and splitback sets.

■ The offensive line is taught how to use the defensive rush technique for a blocking advantage.

Ronnie Haushalter

Fyffe High School

Fyffe, Alabama

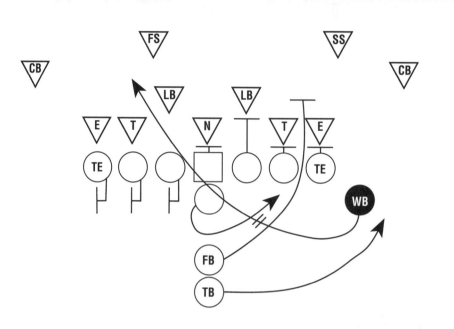

31 Scissors

Play Strategy	Player Assignments	Coaching Points

Play Strategy

This misdirection play is used in all situations. It is often called on third down and long. The play reduces offside pursuit when running basic plays like the FB belly, QB option, and the belly option pass. When running the scissors play, the line uses draw blocking assignments that make it hard for the defense to read.

Player Assignments

Formation: **I-Formation**

Offensive Linemen

RT: Blocks #2 aggressively; allows no penetration.

RG: Blocks #1 aggressively; allows no penetration.

C: Blocks 0 any direction he wants to go.

LG: Steps inside; invites #1 to rush outside. If #1 is LB, leaves and gets upfield block.

LT: Steps inside; invites #2 to rush outside.

Receivers and Backs

LE: Blocks #3 aggressively; allows no penetration.

RE: Steps inside; invites #3 to rush outside.

FB: Runs track at right hip of RT, fakes, and looks for penetration.

LH: Gets in a good pitch relationship with QB.

WB: Lines up 2 yards outside RE, receives outside handoff from QB, and runs to daylight from C to inside the LE.

QB: Reverse pivots, gets depth, puts ball in FB's stomach, and rides him at least 2 steps. After a great fake, hands off outside to WB. He continues to fake the belly.

Coaching Points

■ LG, LT, and LE are taught to set inside so that the DL rushes outside. If not, they take the DL inside.

■ The FB's first step is open right. The QB ball technique is to fake close to his inside arm and shoulder.

■ WB must step back with his inside foot to delay the defense so that the QB has time to ride the FB fake. The WB must time his outside handoff with the QB.

■ It is very important for the QB to shuffle his feet when engaging the FB. He must not force the FB off his track. The QB should look the ball into the WB's stomach.

34

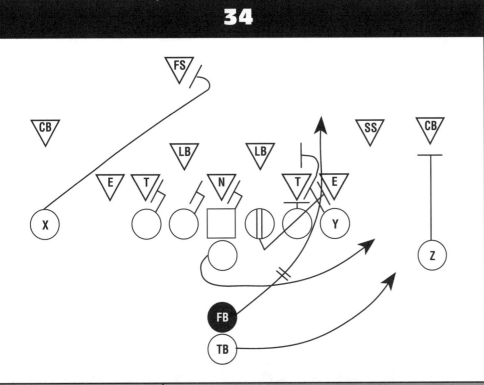

Tom Downing

Wynnewood High School

Wynnewood, Oklahoma

Play Strategy	Player Assignments	Coaching Points

Play Strategy

Coach Downing has built in several options to this play, which may be run out of a one-back set. The play is always run to the TE side.

Player Assignments

Formation: **I-Formation**

Offensive Linemen

PST: Blocks man on, inside.

PSG: Pulls playside; kickout blocks DE. If "covered" rule, PST/TE blocks down.

C: Zone blocks.

BSG: Zone blocks.

BST: Zone blocks.

Receivers and Backs

X: Releases inside; blocks middle 1/3.

Y: Blocks first defender to inside.

Z: Releases downfield; stalk blocks CB.

FB: Aims point at the outside hip of PST, receives handoff, and runs upfield off the combo block of the PST and TE.

TB: Shows pitch; runs the option pitch route.

QB: Reverse pivots, hands off deep to FB, and continues to run corner playside.

Coaching Points

■ Versus 50 defense, the PST and TE combo block. They must be aware of the LB's tendency to scrape outside because he thinks the play is an option.

■ While faking the pitch, the TB is coached to be a good actor. He must draw the attention of the LBs.

■ In a one-back set, the TB aligns with slot left and runs downfield to block the middle third.

■ If PSG can't trap the DE, he runs the option and log blocks him. This is a strong short-yardage play with maximum blocking at POA.

Don Soldinger

**Miami Southridge
High School**

Miami, Florida

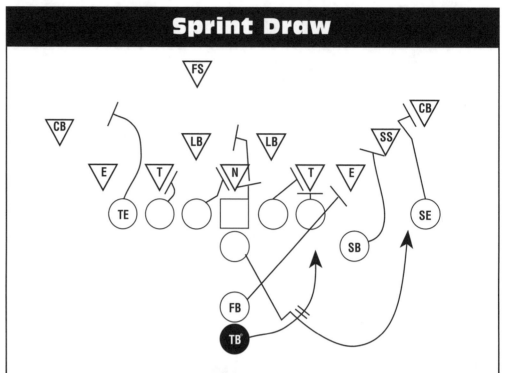

Sprint Draw

Play Strategy	Player Assignments	Coaching Points

Play Strategy

The reaction of the defense to the Sprint Draw is a more important factor than down and distance. The different blocking schemes are used to block the POA more effectively. Versus a 50 front, run it against the tuff LB or run it read may be called. Versus a 60 front, run it or fold it for the backside daylight look may be called. Versus a 70 front, the step it or fold it for the backside are options. Three other plays (the Draw Pass, the Draw Special Protection, and the SE Reverse) complement this all-purpose play.

Player Assignments

Formation: **I-Formation**

Offensive Linemen

PST: Blocks man on; if DT slants, down blocks. If DT stays outside, turnout blocks.

PSG: Steps playside gap upfield to block LB; if slant DT appears, steps around for LB.

C: If covered, blocks Nose; works upfield to block backside LB. If uncovered, blocks middle LB or man on BSG.

BSG: Steps playside gap upfield to block LB; if slant Nose appears, steps around for LB.

BST: If covered, blocks man on; if uncovered, releases inside for near LB.

Receivers and Backs

SE: Releases inside to cut off the CB.

SB: Arc releases to cut off the inside SS.

TE: Releases inside to cut off the backside CB.

FB: Aligns toes at 4-1/2 yards deep, aims at outside hip of PST, and inside-out blocks #3.

TB: Aligns toes at 7-1/2 yards deep; runs read step to inside hip of the SB or the TE, depending on the call. First read is #3 (DE). If #3 pinches, the FB hook blocks, TB runs outside. If #3 sits or comes upfield, TB reads #2 (DT). If #2 maintains outside leverage, TB runs inside. If #2 slants, TB stays outside the PST.

QB: Opens and gets ball deep to TB with short ride; threatens outside.

Coaching Points

■ The teaching progression for introducing this play includes recognition of the defensive fronts, such as the 50, the 60, and the 7 man. Each offensive player is taught the different levels of defenders.

■ Just in case #3 (DE) crosses his face, the FB is drilled on hook blocking.

■ The TB stretches the defense by running in a north/south direction with shoulders parallel to the LOS. This is designed to get the defenders moving in an east/west direction. It forces a defense to be disciplined while moving to the LOS.

25 Sprint Draw

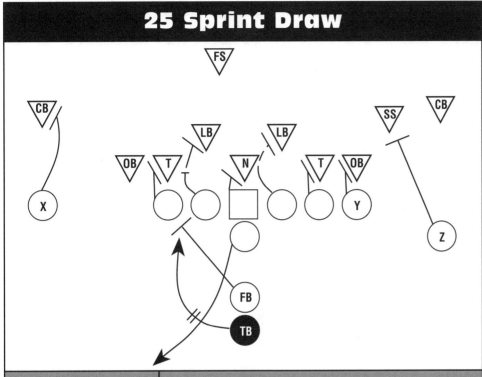

18

John Cooper

Ohio State University

Columbus, Ohio

Big Ten Conference (1A)

Play Strategy

This Sprint Draw is run only to the weak side. It is most often used in a passing down situation. The blast and play action pass are complementary plays for the draw. Coach Cooper runs the play against defenses like the 50 strong, 50 weak, eagle, eagle G, stack, 61 weak, 61 strong, and the buzzard.

Player Assignments

Formation: **I-Formation**

Offensive Linemen

FST: Lead blocks DT.

FSG: If covered, slides and base blocks DT. If uncovered, lead blocks DT.

C: If covered, base blocks the 0 technique (Nose). If uncovered, smash blocks with BSG.

BSG: If covered, base blocks man on. If uncovered, base blocks the 0 technique (Nose).

BST: Stays; cut-off blocks DT.

Receivers and Backs

X: If frontside blocks primary support, backside blocks FS.

Y: If frontside, base blocks DE. If backside, stays and cut-off blocks DE.

Z: Releases downfield; cut-off blocks middle 1/3.

FB: At POA, if FSG is covered, rolls over to block LB. If BSG is uncovered, blocks at inside leg of FST.

TB: Keys FST block. Stays alert for FB blocking rollover.

QB: Opens, hands ball deep to TB, and fakes pass.

Coaching Points

■ On an offset call or when the FSG is covered, the FST does not lead. If facing a read DT, he slide steps to block-5 technique. He must be alert for the smash call (41) from FSG. Versus wide end, he base blocks.

■ When facing an offset Nose, the FSG combo blocks with C. Versus 0 Nose, he makes a "smash" call and executes lead technique. Versus shade Nose or covered, he lead blocks or slide base blocks.

■ Versus offset Nose, C combo blocks with FSG; versus a shade Nose, he smash blocks.

■ Versus shade Nose, the BSG smash blocks with C; versus offset Nose, he cut-off blocks half on inside defender.

■ After the handoff, the QB drops back to set up for a fake pass.

■ Linemen are asked to take maximum splits.

19

Dennis Kozlowski

Bethel High School

Hampton, Virginia

Jumbo Right 76 Read

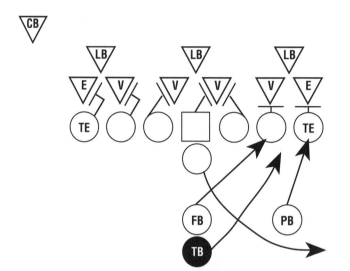

Play Strategy

This play is called when inside the 10-yard line or to gain a first down in a short-yardage situation. The defense is challenged by this utilization of the best back principle behind power blocking at the POA.

Player Assignments

Formation: **Power I-Formation**

Offensive Linemen

RT: Blocks DT any direction.

RG: Lead steps left; blocks #1 defensive guard.

C: Leads right; prevents penetration by defensive guard or LB.

LG: Blocks defensive LG; cuts off inside penetration and pursuit.

LT: Blocks defensive LT; cuts off inside penetration and pursuit.

Receivers and Backs

RTE: Blocks DE any direction.

LTE: Blocks inside; cuts off inside penetration and pursuit.

FB: Reads the RT's block. If he blocks DT down, goes outside off his tail and seals off LB.

PB (powerback): Reads RTE's block. If he blocks DE down, PB goes outside his tail and blocks either LB or CB.

TB: Attacks the LOS following FB and PB; waits for seam to appear (in or out) and accelerates.

QB: Fronts out, hands ball deep to TB, and runs away.

Coaching Points

■ Both the RT and the RTE block the assigned defender any way he wants to go. They must sustain their blocks.

■ Offensive linemen are coached to stop penetration by the defensive front.

■ Mistakes are kept to a minimum due to the simplicity of running off-tackle.

■ While on the move, the FB and PB (powerback) blocking combination read the blocks of the RT and RTE, respectively.

■ The TB keys the blocking combination, picks the first seam that opens, and runs either inside or outside.

■ Presnap reads of the defense by the linemen and backs usually tell them who to block. The read also tells the TB which seam will open.

Wedge 2nd Man

Dick Tighe

Webster City High School

Webster City, Iowa

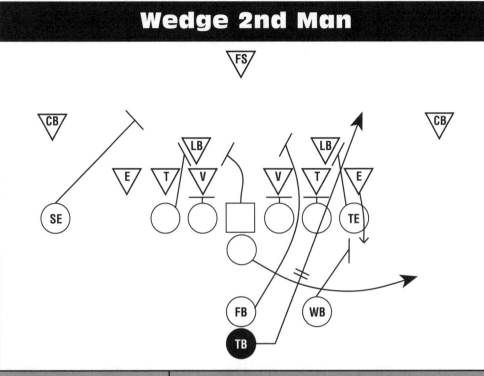

Play Strategy

This play is a natural companion to the wedge play. It is called in short or long situations. It is a better play when the FB has been having a good day rushing and can use the fake inside for deception. The play is essentially the same as the old inside belly series except it is run out of I-Formation. The WB may choose to line up at the wing spot rather than in the backfield. Coach Tighe believes that the Wedge 2nd Man works better when the wedge play has been successful.

Player Assignments

Formation: **Power I-Formation**

Offensive Linemen

WT: Releases inside gap; blocks downfield.

WG: If covered, blocks man over; if uncovered, blocks LB over.

C: If covered, blocks Nose; if uncovered, blocks backside LB.

SG: If covered, blocks man over; if uncovered, blocks LB over.

ST: Blocks man over.

Receivers and Backs

SE: Releases inside to block downfield.

TE: Releases inside; blocks LB or man in gap.

FB: Fakes quickly over SG; becomes blocker.

WB: Blocks out on first man outside TE.

TB: Steps lateral 1 step, drives off outside leg, takes handoff, and sprints to the off-tackle hole.

QB: Takes 1 step back, fakes ball to FB, steps out wide with right foot, rides ball to TB, and fakes keeper playside.

Coaching Points

■ The footwork and ball handling of the FB and QB look exactly as they do for the wedge. After the good ride fake, the QB steps back and reaches for the TB. The key to the whole play is the FB's timing.

■ After a lateral step, the TB rounds off his move forward to the POA by using choppy steps. He shouldn't hurry his approach until he has the ball. This controlled delay gives the QB time to execute a good FB fake and bring the ball deep to the TB.

■ The line blocking is the same as for the belly series, which helps to promote consistency.

Tam Hollingshead

Permian High School

Odessa, Texas

(1990–1993)

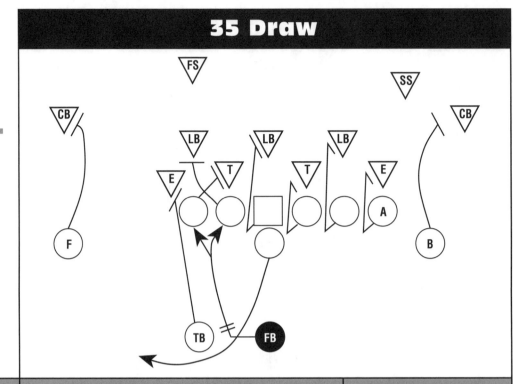

35 Draw

Play Strategy

Coach Hollingshead's draw play is used in passing situations. The play is set up by running the sprint-out passing game. There are four different ways to block the POA, so they play can be called against almost any defense.

Player Assignments

Formation: **Wing-T**

Offensive Linemen

TT: Shows pass; blocks over, LB.

TG: Shows pass; blocks over, LB.

C: Shows pass; blocks Nose, LB.

SG: Blocks over, LB; reads "David" vs. 40 or 80 defense.

ST: Blocks over; possibly reads "David" vs. 40 or 80 defense.

Receivers and Backs

A: Zip gate; vs. cheat, blocks out.

B: Drives; stalk blocks CB.

F: Drives; stalk blocks CB.

TB: Runs to block inside out on DE.

FB: Takes lead step crossover, squares up, and takes handoff.

QB: Sprints out and executes handoff to FB deep; runs the corner.

Coaching Points

■ It is important for the backside linemen to show pass before applying the blocking rule.

■ SG and ST switch assignments when they read man on SG. ST blocks down; SG releases inside or around to block near LB.

■ Unless he sees gut, the TB is taught to set up passively and not to attack the DE.

■ After receiving the handoff, the FB reads the POA to run inside or outside.

■ The QB's sprint out must look like he is going to pass. This is vital to the execution of the draw.

983 XBL

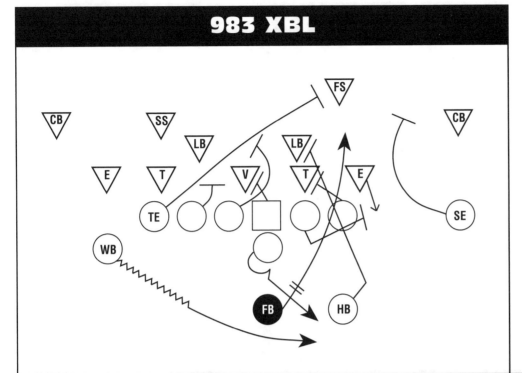

Art Fiore

LaSalle Academy

Providence, Rhode Island

Play Strategy

The play is run on any down and distance situation from 1st and 10 to 3rd and long. The primary play is to establish the belly attack, which is used to establish dominance on the LOS. The belly is a simple play that can be run against any defense. As a result, the play can be called anywhere on the field.

Player Assignments

Formation: **Wing-T**

Offensive Linemen

ONT: Blocks gap, down, on.

ONG: Pulls onside; blocks out on the first man outside of the ONT.

C: Reach blocks, on, LB.

OFG: Reach blocks, on, LB.

OFT: Reach blocks, on, LB.

Receivers and Backs

SE: Onside, fakes crackback block, walls off inside. Offside, cut-off blocks downfield.

WB: Leaves in 3-step motion and fakes keep pass.

TE: Onside, blocks first LB inside. Offside, cut-off blocks downfield.

HB: Onside, steps out, dives for the tail of the ONT, reads tail of ONT, blocks first LB from C. Offside, leaves in 3-step motion and fakes keep pass.

FB: Lead steps, crosses over, on third step bends path for the inside foot of the ONT, receives handoff from QB, reads first down lineman from C.

QB: Reverse pivots, first step on midline, second step 45 degrees over midline, hands off to FB, fakes keep pass.

Coaching Points

■ Onside HB reads the block of the ONT to decide whether to go inside or outside to block the LB. He is coached to block the LB at hip level, where he bends.

■ Offside HB leaves in early motion (3-step) and attacks the flank.

■ The FB is in a 2-point stance, aware of the blocking scheme at POA. While bending, he receives the ball from the QB (on his third step) and reads the block of the ONT. He must be aware of cutback opportunities.

■ When executing gap or down technique, the ONT uses a bucket step, not a lead step. He makes initial contact with reverse-shoulder technique. If the defender is reading, the ONT uses the near-shoulder technique and puts his head on the upfield side.

■ On his reverse pivot, the QB lets his head come around on the pivot. He must avoid stepping too flat on his second step or the FB may be forced too wide. The QB always works with tight elbows and bends at the waist, which helps in faking and in hiding the ball from the defense.

■ The first uncovered lineman on the backside makes an "odd" call. The adjacent linemen step under and come up to the LB. An exception is when there is the threat of a LB run-through.

■ First digit (formation), second digit (series), third digit (hole number), plus suffix helps to modify the blocking assignment (cross block).

Sonny Lubick

Colorado State University

Fort Collins, Colorado

Western Conference (1A)

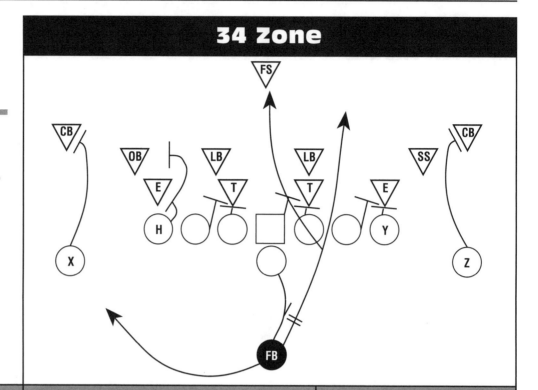

34 Zone

Play Strategy	Player Assignments	Coaching Points

Play Strategy

In addressing different defensive fronts, you can run the 34 Zone on any down. It is most effective in short-yardage situations when used to pick up a first down. The fact that the QB runs the bootleg away keeps the backside DE occupied. The cutback adds another dimension that will concern defensive coordinators.

Player Assignments

Formation: **One-Back**

Offensive Linemen

ST: "Trike" call: steps outside gap; works upfield to block LB. "Take" call: Blocks outside gap on LOS with Y.

SG: "Base" call: blocks man on. "Solid" call: blocks outside gap on LOS. "Combo" call: blocks man on with help from ST.

C: "Base" call: blocks Nose. "Ram" call: blocks playside gap on LOS. "Lion" call: blocks playside gap on LOS. "City" call: blocks playside gap on LOS.

WG and WT: "Solid" call: block playside gap on LOS. "Base" call: block man on.

Receivers and Backs

X: Releases upfield; stalk blocks CB.

Z: Releases upfield; stalk blocks CB.

Y: Blocks man on; "take" call: be alert for outside defender on LOS.

H: Steps inside to cut off first down defender from WT to outside.

FB: Runs belly action, aims at the outside hip of the SG, and receives handoff.

QB: Opens to 5:30 with belly action; fakes bootleg.

Coaching Points

■ Depending on the defensive front, the line makes two-to-three calls to control the LOS. Get maximum push on down defenders on all zone and combo blocks. Coach line to be physical and knock defenders off the LOS.

■ Y must aim for the outside and keep his shoulders parallel to LOS. Y uses maximum force to knock the defender off the LOS and stays alert for the pinch.

■ After receiving the handoff, the FB runs at the first down defensive lineman on the SG. If the first down lineman is on the ST, the FB can veer at the ST's inside hip.

■ The FB must make his cuts on the LOS with quickness and explode upfield with force.

■ If the H-Back is in the slot, (thunder) stalk blocks the coverage defender.

■ The QB gives the FB room and doesn't force him wide. If the plays are called left, the QB opens at 6 o'clock.

35 Zone

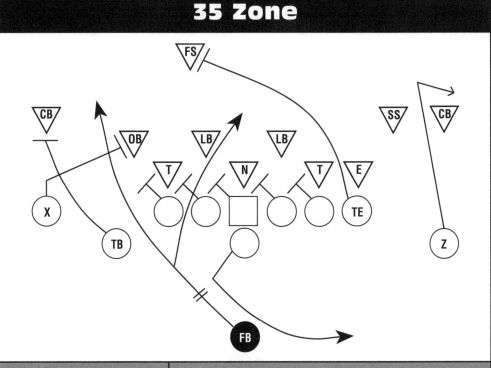

Chuck Tarbox

Eastside Catholic High School

Bellevue, Washington

Play Strategy

The 35 Zone is used to establish the running game, especially to set up plays like the counter-trey, countergap, and bootleg. Using the same blocking scheme, Coach Tarbox may also run the A back in counter action. Although it can be run on any down, this play is most often used on a first down. The defense is forced to deal with four receivers and horizontal stretching.

Player Assignments

Formation: **One-Back**

Offensive Linemen

ST: Zone steps to cut off #2.

SG: Zone steps #1 and 0 with C.

C: Zone steps 0 and #1 with SG.

QG: Zone steps #1 and #2 with QT.

QT: Zone steps #2 and #1 with QG.

Receivers and Backs

X: Slants inside to block OB in walk-off position or blocks second level to COF (coaching on field).

Z: Blocks deep 1/3 or man on.

TE: CFBP (cross field blocking point) at the FS.

FB: Takes crossover step, receives handoff from QB, and runs slice or cutback.

TB: (Ace) vs. OB (whip) in walk-off position; wheels and blocks CB. Blocks OB on LOS.

QB: Opens at 4 o'clock, hands ball off to FB, and fakes boot strong side.

Coaching Points

■ At the POA, X and A sight adjust the position of the QB (whip) to determine whom to block. If the QB is up on LOS, A blocks solid. If necessary, a "check with me" call may be used.

■ Depending on what opens, the FB has the option of running the slice or cutback.

■ The threat of a QB boot keeps the backside DE occupied.

■ The QB learns to sit on the fake, and then run the boot with speed.

■ The slot set forces the OB (whip) to stay in under coverage or line up on the LOS.

25

Eric Roanhaus

Clovis High School

Clovis, New Mexico

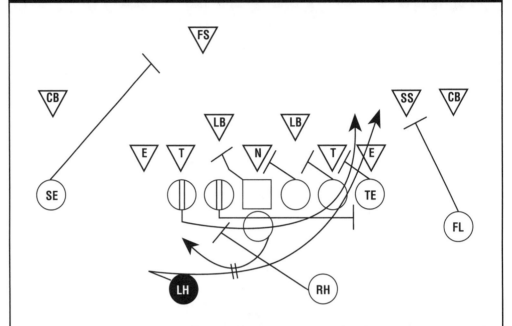

42 Counter Trap

Play Strategy	Player Assignments	Coaching Points

Play Strategy

Coach Roanhaus likes to use this play against overshifted and attacking defenses. The play can be run toward the TE side or the open side from multiple formations such as twins, slot, and trips. Complementary plays include the QB keeper and a play action pass off the countertrap. The play can be run from the Pro set, Twins, Slot, or Trips formations.

Player Assignments

Formation: **Split Backs**

Offensive Linemen

PST: If covered, blocks man on solid. If uncovered, blocks down.

PSG: If covered, blocks man on. If uncovered, blocks down on Nose.

C: Blocks backside gap.

BSG: Pulls down the line. Kickout blocks the 9 (DE) or 7 (DT).

BST: Pulls down the line; turns up first soft spot and goal inside. If no defender there, goes to the next level.

Receivers and Backs

SE: Stalk blocks the middle 1/3

TE: With defender on and one outside, blocks out. If not, blocks down.

FL: Stalk blocks outside 1/3.

RH: Steps with inside foot, fills for pulling BST.

LH: Takes a counterstep and receives a backside handoff from QB.

QB: Opens to hole, fakes to RH, and hands off to LH.

Coaching Points

■ To locate soft spot to turn upfield, the pulling BST must read the block of the BSG while on the move.

■ Line cuts down splits to 18 inches, which helps to seal off penetration.

■ LH's counterstep includes the turning of his shoulders upfield.

■ The better the fake to the offback, the better the execution of the counter-trap.

Split Right Switch Motion Left 56

Gil Rector

Lexington High School

Lexington, Missouri

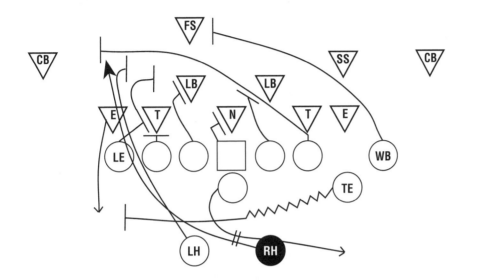

Play Strategy	Player Assignments	Coaching Points

Play Strategy

Companion plays include the quick pitch, quick trap inside, bootleg pass, and sprint pass. The TE motion scheme puts pressure on the defense in short-yardage situations, especially on second or third down. If the defense commits because of motion, a big play potential is possible. Play strategy depends on how the defense handles the TE's motion.

Player Assignments

Formation: **Split Backs**

Offensive Linemen

LT: Blocks man on; if the DT loops outside, he must have help from LE.

LG: Sprints to the left playside hip of LB; maintains contact.

C: Reach blocks Nose.

RG: Sprints to playside hip of LB; maintains contact.

RT: Releases inside DT; sprints to block downfield (10 yards upfield playside).

Receivers and Backs

LE: Double-team blocks with LT. If DT disappears, blocks LB upfield.

WB: Releases inside; sprints downfield to block the FS.

TE: Goes in motion behind the QB. On snap, blocks out playside DE.

LH: Lead blocks; aims at outside hip of LT. Looks inside to block LB, looks outside for CB, or runs downfield to block near safety.

RH: Follows lead blocker (FB); runs at POA.

QB: Reverse pivots, locks ball in, and carries out bootleg.

Coaching Points

■ The ball is snapped precisely when the TE is directly behind the QB. This allows the TE to explode toward the DE at full speed. He keeps his head inside, makes contact, and drives the DE off the LOS.

■ While following the lead blocker, the BC's shoulder pads should be square to the LOS.

■ The TE and WB exchange positions when "switch" is called. The TE/WB splits remain the same.

■ The play may be run to both the strong and weak side without having to change blocking assignments.

■ The play is run from the Wing-I or Wing Split Backs formations.

27

Rocky Hager

North Dakota State University

Fargo, North Dakota

North Central Conference (1AA)

46 Veer

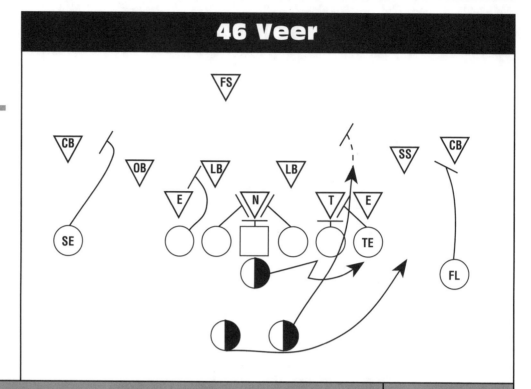

Play Strategy

Coach Hager's favorite play, the 46 Veer is run from goal line to goal line. It can be called in any situation. This wide-open play spreads defensive coverages, and the triple option especially threatens the defensive secondary. The play's strength comes from the quarterback's ability to read his keys. He can hand off to the DB, run with the ball off-tackle, or pitch to the trailing back. Defending the option is tough enough, but defending a triple is even more demanding.

Player Assignments

Formation: **Veer**

Offensive Linemen

PST: Versus "Okie" call, double teams #5 technique DT. Versus "over" call, double teams #4 or #5 technique DT. Versus 40 call, either blocks downs on #3 technique DT or triple teams #2 technique DT.

PSG: Versus "Okie" call, triple teams 0 technique Nose. Versus "over" call, double teams #2 technique DT. Versus 40 call, triple teams #2 technique DT or X blocks to playside threat.

C: Versus "Okie" call, triple teams 0 technique Nose. Versus "over" call, double teams #2 technique DT. Versus 40 call, triple teams #2 technique DT or releases to BSL backside LB.

BSG: Versus "Okie" call, triple teams 0 technique Nose. Versus "over" call, releases to backside LB. Versus 40 call, cut blocks backside #1 technique Nose.

BST: Versus "Okie" call, releases inside and cuts off first threat. Versus "over" call, cuts #3 technique DT. Versus 40 call, releases inside and cuts off first threat.

Receivers and Backs

SE: Runs backside; cuts off onside CB.

TE: Versus "Okie" call, double teams #5 technique DT. Versus "over" call, double teams #4 or #5 technique DT. Versus 40 call, veer releases to FS.

FL: Versus "Okie" call, stalks CB; seals sideline for pitch. Versus "over" call, slams to CB and releases to SS.

DB: Versus "Okie" or "over" call, tracks to double team PST or TE. Versus 40 call, tracks to inside hip of PST.

PB: Keeps pitch relationship; receives pitch running downhill.

QB: COF (coached on field)

Coaching Points

■ The QB is coached to read all triple options by using a number system labeled the *1-2-3 rule.*

■ The QB reads #1 (first defender on or outside PST). If the defender sits or widens, the QB gives the ball to DB. Should he close to dive, the QB pulls and hustles to #2. If the DE runs to cover the PB, the QB runs upfield and stretches the field as he runs the perimeter. He reacts to the TE's block on the FS. If the DE attacks the QB, he pitches the ball to the PB.

T36 Power

John Jenkins

Newton High School

Newton, Iowa

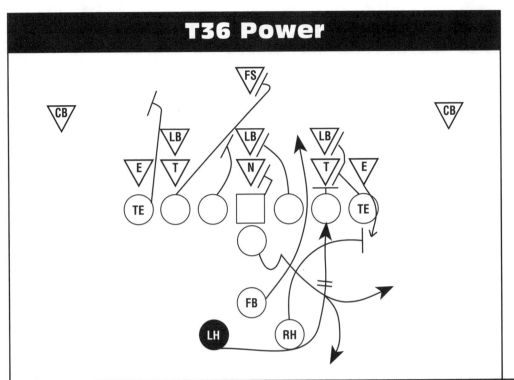

Play Strategy	Player Assignments	Coaching Points

Play Strategy

The T36 Power is used in any situation, even on third or fourth down and long. Coach Jenkins runs this play against defenses that have loosened up, expecting a pass. Another wrinkle is to run the play toward the split side or use double slots, in which one lead blocks for the other.

Player Assignments

Formation: **Bone**

Offensive Linemen

PST: Combo blocks with PSTE the DT, reads the LB, and may release to block. Base blocks defender on.

PSG: If covered, doesn't allow defender on to cross face. Versus 5-3, seal blocks the middle LB. Versus 5-2, blocks the near LB.

C: Steps to insure the playside gap seal.

BSG: If covered, prevents defender on to cross face. If uncovered, seal blocks the weakside LB.

BST: Releases hard inside flat to position block the FS.

Receivers and Backs

PSTE: Combo blocks the DT; releases to seal block the LB. May stay with the block and have PST release to seal block the LB.

BSTE: Releases hard inside toward the FS. If possible, blocks him. If chasing wheels and seal blocks the BSCB.

FB: Drives at the PSG's outside hip. Fakes handoff.

RH: Blocks the first defender to show outside the DE.

LH: Runs parallel to the LOS; receives handoff from QB. When he reaches the PSG-PST guard, he squares up his shoulder and attacks the LOS.

QB: Steps playside at 45 degrees, rides the FB for step, pulls ball, gives ball to LH on second step, then runs the playside keeper or backside bootleg.

Coaching Points

■ Against a base-52 defense, the PSG must block the LB.

■ BST must focus and punch through the FS's numbers, and never look for the ball.

■ FB forms a pocket with his inside elbow up, thumb down on sternum, outside elbow down with arm, and hand forming a cradle. The FB redirects his focus on the PSG's block, to help sell the fake.

■ RH's most difficult task is to not block too soon. The first step is made with his left foot forward, and then on his third "slow" step, he turns out to block the DE.

■ LH reads the POA, looks for a seam. It's important that he stay inside. He takes the handoff and accelerates upfield, needing to beat only the playside CB for a TD.

■ The QB brings the ball to his belly, dropsteps with his playside foot at a 45-degree angle. He looks the ball into the FB's pocket, and rides him for 1 full step. He pulls the ball out, uses a drive step deep toward the LH, and gives the ball on the second deep step to the LH. After the handoff, the QB focuses on the most dangerous defender on the keeper or bootleg side.

Alan Chadwick

Marist School

Atlanta, Georgia

Red 34 Belly

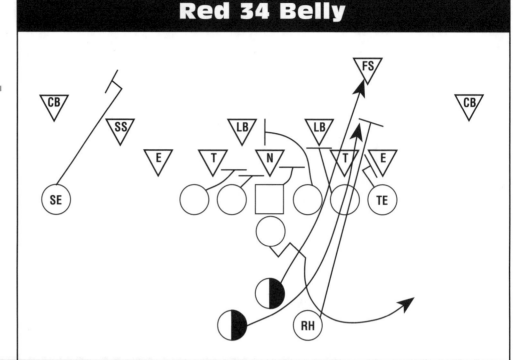

Play Strategy	Player Assignments	Coaching Points

Play Strategy

This play is called in any situation except 3rd and 6+. The play is often called on 3rd and 5+ or 4th and 5+. Coach Chadwick likes to run this play for finesse, not for power. The advantages of the play include not having to block the read man at the POA and, as an added blocker, the FB picks up stunts by the scrape LB. The play is good against any defensive front (i.e., in the open field, in short yardage, or in goal-line situations).

Player Assignments

Formation: **Bone**

Offensive Linemen

RT: Steps with inside foot and blocks B gap; pushes upfield to block LB.

RG: Combos A gap with C if C calls for help. If C does not call for help, RG steps with outside foot (6 inches) to B gap and blocks LB.

C: Calls for help from RG if needed. Steps with playside foot, tries to cut off Nose. If C combos with RG, may rub off and block backside LB on pursuit pattern.

LG: Blocks backside scoop, blocks backside A gap, or pushes upfield to block.

LT: Blocks backside scoop, blocks backside B gap, or pushes upfield to block.

Receivers and Backs

SE: Releases to angle block CB.

TE: Steps 6 inches with inside foot; executes a turnout block on the DE.

FB: Runs mesh track, aiming at outside hip of RG.

RH: Runs alley block at right hip of RT. If DT works outside, RH blocks his outside hip. If DT closes inside RH, looks inside for LB on scrape outside. If LB shows outside, RH collisions LB. If LB does not show, RH upfield blocks CB or FS.

LH: Steps right parallel to LOS, takes left step to hole (outside hip of RT). Makes a pocket to receive handoff. Continues even if FB gets ball.

QB: Opens steps at 45 degrees to mesh with FB. Reads DT as he rides with FB. Gives to FB or LH.

Coaching Points

■ Versus a 4-3 defense, the TE blocks the defensive man responsible for the D gap.

■ If the DE closes or pinches inside, the TE drives him past POA.

■ The only time the lead RH varies his track is when the DE slants inside. Then he looks for the first defender outside the TE's downblock.

■ The TE must step with his inside foot to avoid getting beaten to the C gap by the DE.

■ The QB reads only the DT. If the DT or read man lines up inside the OT, it is automatically a second handoff. If the DT works upfield or does not commit to the FB, the ball is handed off. If the DT closes down or takes the FB, the QB pulls the ball and gives to the LH (second back).

T36

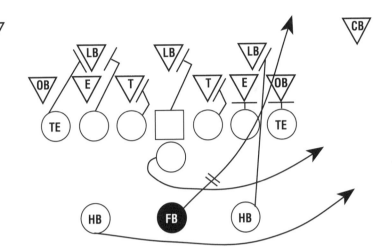

Timothy Jaureguito

South Tahoe High School

South Lake Tahoe, California

Play Strategy	Player Assignments	Coaching Points

Play Strategy

The play T36 is most often used as a goal-line or short-yardage play. It is, however, effective at any point in the game, anywhere on the field. This power play's success depends on an effective use of the option and play-action pass to counteract the strength of the defense. Coach Jaureguito believes this whole package is difficult to defend, especially in the red zone.

Player Assignments

Formation: **Fullhouse**

Offensive Linemen

FST: 2 call, base blocks man on. 6 call, post blocks on double team with TE. "Gap-gap" call, blocks the first defender to inside.

FSG: 2 call: vs. even, reach blocks #1. Versus odd, blocks lead LB. 6 call: vs. even, reach blocks #2. Versus odd, blocks lead LB. "Gap-gap" call, scoop blocks with C.

C: Reach blocks frontside gap. Versus even, blocks lead LB. "Gap-gap" call, scoop blocks #1 frontside.

BSG: Reach blocks frontside gap.

BST: Runs inside release frontside gap, shallow blocks crossfield.

Receivers and Backs

FSTE: 2 call, base blocks man on. 6 call, double-team blocks with PST. "Gap-gap" call, blocks first defender to inside.

BSTE: Runs inside release frontside gap, shallow blocks crossfield.

FSB: 2 call, reads tackles block to LB.

BSB: Sprints frontside; sells the option.

FB: Takes lead step frontside, aims for middle of PST, receives handoff from QB, and runs low.

QB: Reverses out, extends arms, rides FB, hands ball off, and continues option course around end.

Coaching Points

- Even though the play is designed for use in short-yardage offense, line splits are base, not reduced.

- It is a must to get movement at the POA.

- The lead back's block at the POA is critical to the success of the play.

- A FB with quickness and power is a plus to running this off-tackle play.

- QB must sell the option with BSB.

Harold R. "Tubby" Raymond

University of Delaware

Newark, Delaware

Yankee Conference
(1AA)

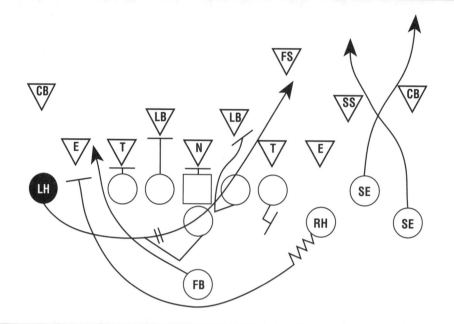

89 Sally at 3

Play Strategy

Coach Raymond's unbalanced misdirectional play is not usually seen in the Wing-T offense. This play may be used at any time, but it is most often called when the element of surprise is needed. It also may be used as a first-down call. The defense has difficulty making an adjustment because line blocking indicates a pass and not a run. Another option calls for the play to be used as a draw.

Player Assignments

Formation: **Trips**

Offensive Linemen

The numbering system is right to left, 1 to 9 with the C #5.

ONT: Aggressively blocks down or man on.

ONG: Aggressively blocks defender on or inside gap.

C: If covered, blocks defender on. If uncovered, sets up in cup protection as if to show pass.

OFG: Sets up in cup protection as if to show pass.

OFT: Sets up in cup protection as if to show pass.

Receivers and Backs

SE: Outside receiver releases outside; turns inside for the SS running a crossing pattern.

SE: Inside receiver releases directly at the CB; blocks or runs off in a crossing pattern.

FB: Runs belly track; fakes ride with QB.

RH: Goes in motion behind the TB; blocks DE.

LH: Jabs steps, gets depth, and receives inside handoff from QB.

QB: Reverse pivots, fakes ride with FB, hands off inside to LH.

Coaching Points

- This unbalanced formation uses two spread ends in the game at the same time. There is no TE.

- The LH lines up on the LOS. He is split from the OFT. His alignment is opposite the trips.

- With this spread look, a defense must prepare to defend horizontally rather than against the usual closed Wing-T formations.

- Important for LH to take delayed step.

46 Toss

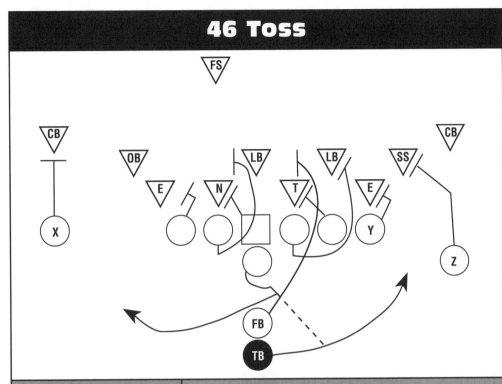

Bobby Bowden

Florida State University

Tallahassee, Florida

Atlantic Coast Conference (1A)

Play Strategy

Coach Bowden has high expectations for this play. It can be run on any down anywhere on the field. Different blocking schemes can be used against defenses like stack 4, stack 3-G, 8-man, 22, 33, 44, 53, 54, and other fronts that crowd the LOS. This play has gained plus yardage throughout Coach Bowden's career.

Player Assignments

Formation: **I-Formation**

Offensive Linemen

TT: Blocks DT. Versus slack 3-G, blocks strong B gap.

TG: Pulls playside; blocks support (SS). "Crack" call, blocks CB; vs. stack 3-G, blocks Sam LB.

C: Scoop blocks strong A gap to backside LB. Versus stack 3-G, blocks Charlie Weak Nose.

SG: Scoop blocks A gap.

ST: Scoop blocks B gap.

Receivers and Backs

X: Versus Will Hawk runs outside release, blocks CB.

Y: Blocks man on.

Z: Blocks CB. If CB goes deep, blocks SS (cover 3 and 1)

FB: Drives for inside leg of TT, runs 34 landmark track strong, and blocks strongside LB.

TB: Takes a slow, flat step strong side, receives pitch from QB, reads Y's block, and runs downhill.

QB: Reverse pivots, pitches to TB going strong, and fakes naked boot.

Coaching Points

■ Every defender is blocked on the snap of the ball, even against stems or blitzes.

■ The TB looks the ball into his hands. After reading Y's block, he reacts accordingly with speed and quickness.

■ Versus stack, the FB must look inside to block the middle LB (Mike).

■ Y must maintain contact with blocking man on. He must be prepared to handle the crashing or skating end.

33

Chuck Mizerski

Lincoln-Southeast
High School

Lincoln, Nebraska

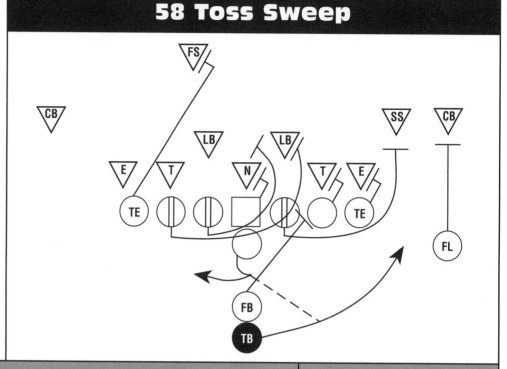

58 Toss Sweep

Play Strategy

The 58 Toss Sweep, Coach Mizerski's basic outside play, strengthens his running game. Because multiple blocking schemes are in place to run the play, it may be run in any given situation against any defense. The double-tight formation forces the defense to be balanced in order to stop the run.

Player Assignments

Formation: **I-Formation**

Offensive Linemen

RT: Blocks left seam, on, right seam, or LB. Versus 4-3 spacing, blocks man on RG; makes 5 call to C. Blocks defenders in both seams, makes 2 call, then blocks inside. If stack is called, locks on.

RG: Pulls right, looks to block force man. Versus stack or 4-3, blocks OLB.

C: Blocks right, on, or LB. Versus eagle or stack, makes 6 call; blocks onside LB.

LG: Blocks right seam, on, or backside LB. Versus stack, scoop blocks man on with LT.

LT: Pulls right, blocks first man to show downfield. Versus stack, scoop blocks on LG.

Receivers and Backs

TE: ONTE: Blocks on, right, or LB. Aims at outside number of defender. OFTE: Blocks right seam; cuts off FS.

FL: Releases downfield, blocks first deep man, and blocks force vs. stack.

FB: Aims at inside hip of RT; blocks first man to cross his face.

TB: Receives toss from QB, reads the blocking of the pulling RG, and runs upfield.

QB: Reverse pivots, tosses to TB, and checks backside to run or block.

Coaching Points

■ If covered, the RT executes a rip-reach block. He leans on the defender and maintains contact. If uncovered, the RT blocks down. He steps at a 45-degree angle with his left foot and aims his helmet upfield behind the defender.

■ Upon reaching the force man, the RG executes a good lift with his hands. He sprints through and over the defender.

■ The C uses a rip-reach technique when blocking the Nose. If blocking playside defender, he executes a scramble block on all fours and works upfield after contact.

■ If uncovered, the LG steps around the Nose to block the backside LB. If blocking the Nose, the LG executes a pull step with his right foot and overtakes the Nose. Versus a stack, the LG executes the rip-reach technique.

41 Pitch

34

Tom Osborne

University of Nebraska

Lincoln, Nebraska

Big Eight Conference
(1A)

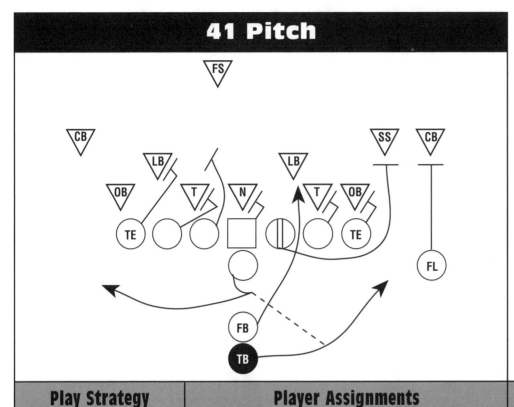

Play Strategy

This is Nebraska's #1 football play. It can be called at any time or any place on the field. This play damages defenses more than any other because of the emphasis placed on coaching each position. It is a popular model for short yardage and when the team desperately needs a first down. The play can be run against defenses such as wide tackle, stack, eagle, bear, or others that mix up containment responsibilities.

Player Assignments

Formation: **I-Formation**

Offensive Linemen

RT: Blocks left seam, on, right seam, LB.

RG: Pulls right, thinks outside force man, and blocks LB vs. stack or 4-3.

C: Blocks right, on, LB.

LG: Blocks right, seam, on, backside LB.

LT: Pulls right; as soon as congestion is cleared goes upfield and blocks first man to show downfield.

Receivers and Backs

ONTE: Blocks on, right, LB.

OFTE: Blocks right seam, cuts off, blocks FS.

ONFL: Blocks first deep man; blocks force vs. stack.

FB: Aims at the inside hip of RT; blocks first man to cross path.

TB: Receives end-over-end pitch from QB; reads the pulling RG's block on the force defender.

QB: Reverses out, tosses to TB, and checks backside.

Coaching Points

■ Blocking rules and calls help the offensive linemen determine their blocking assignments against defensive fronts.

■ Linemen blocking calls create better blocking schemes: 5 *call* by RT blocks man on RG; the C makes the 6 *call* vs. MG, stack, or eagle, blocks the onside gap, and the 2 *call* by the RT is made vs. man in both seams, so he blocks inside.

■ LT scoop blocks a stack on the LG.

■ If no linemen come up free, the FB running inside bounces for the LB.

35

Barry Alvarez

University of
Wisconsin

Madison, Wisconsin

Big Ten Conference (1A)

38 Option

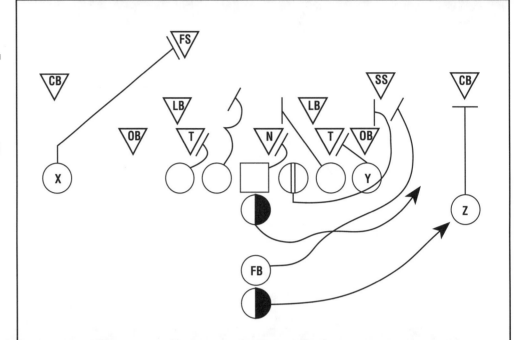

Play Strategy	Player Assignments	Coaching Points

Play Strategy

This two-way option play is called during normal situations, regardless of down and distance. The twin and pro sets offer another look, which causes a defense to make adjustments. In short yardage situations, two TEs may be brought in to balance the attack. Another option is to run the same play with short Z motion or Z motion across the formation.

Player Assignments

Formation: **I-Formation**

Offensive Linemen

PST: Blocks inside gap down to backside LB.

PSG: Pulls; log blocks EMOL.

C: Blocks playside A gap to backside LB.

BSG: Scoop blocks playside.

BST: Scoop blocks playside.

Receivers and Backs

X: Blocks backside near safety.

Z: If playside vs. cover 3, blocks man on; vs. cover 2, blocks near safety. If backside, blocks near safety.

Y: If playside, track blocks first man inside to backside LB. If backside, scoop blocks.

FB: Sets heels at 5 yards, jab steps abort fake, and seal blocks first inside LB playside.

HB: Sets heels at 7 yards, jab steps away, and phases with QB as long as possible.

QB: Reverses out deep; gets shoulders downhill to #4.

Coaching Points

■ PST is coached to take a drop step and rip through #5 technique tackle. He must be alert to help 0 shade Nose.

■ PSG must wrap it tight on log blocking EMOL; works to block LB to FS.

■ While blocking the A gap, C must not allow penetration.

■ The QB must think sprint and get away while the HB is phasing 5 yards deep, 1 yard ahead of QB.

■ The QB may pitch immediately to the HB or may pitch downfield.

■ If the FB is in motion or sets wide, he must avoid the chop crack block.

Belly Option

36

Mack Brown

University of North Carolina

Chapel Hill, North Carolina

Atlantic Coast Conference (1A)

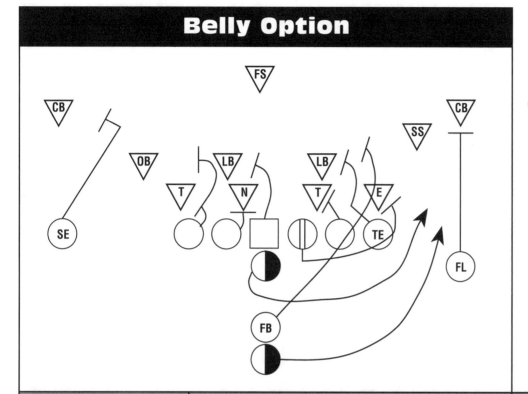

Play Strategy	Player Assignments	Coaching Points

Play Strategy

Coach Brown calls the Belly Option at any time. The play is helped by a complementary power play in which the FB runs off-tackle and is effective when run to the TE side. The double-option play run off the FB puts pressure on containment.

Player Assignments

Formation: **I-Formation**

Offensive Linemen

ONT: If guard is covered, blocks down on all techniques. If guard is uncovered, combo blocks with TE to LB.

ONG: Pulls and log blocks DE or seal blocks on LB inside.

C: Blocks 0 through backside gap.

OFG: Cutoff blocks #1 backside.

OFT: Cutoff blocks #2 backside.

Receivers and Backs

SE: Blocks backside 1/3 or 1/2.

TE: Gap blocks down to first inside LB.

FL: Stalk blocks the CB.

FB: Executes belly; blocks playside LB through or around.

TB: Sprints to sideline; keeps pitch relationship with QB.

QB: Reverse pivots flat to LOS, courtesy fake to FB, clears LOS, and options #4.

Coaching Points

■ The TB must maintain a pitch relationship with the QB and expect the pitch to occur at any time.

■ It is important that this relationship is maintained, because the pitch can occur 10 to 12 yards downfield.

■ The LOS must be secured so that the QB can pitch off #4 by crossing the LOS.

■ The ONG's log block on the DE is critical. It allows the QB to get to #4.

■ Because the TE blocks inside, option responsibilities are changed.

37

Herb Deromedi

Central Michigan University

Mount Pleasant, Michigan

(1978–1993)

Mid-American Conference

Toss Sweep Right

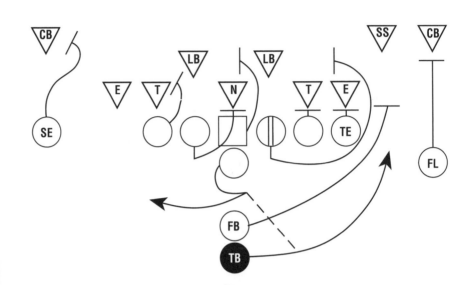

Play Strategy	Player Assignments	Coaching Points
Depending on the soft spots in the defense, this bread and butter play may be run on any given down. When reading the FB's block, the depth of TB has short- and long-yardage potential. Coach Deromedi runs his inside/outside toss sweep in either direction.	Formation: **I-Formation** **Offensive Linemen** **FST:** Hook blocks man on; down blocks. **FSG:** Pulls frontside; looks to block LB or FS. **C:** Over scoops frontside; blocks man on. **BSG:** Over scoops frontside. **BST:** Rips through DT. **Receivers and Backs** **SE:** Blocks CB downfield. **FL:** Blocks CB downfield. **TE:** Frontside, blocks base; backside, blocks crossfield. **FB:** Reads block of TE; runs inside or outside to block SS force. **TB:** Dropsteps with foot opposite called side, catches pitch running downhill, and follows block of FB. **QB:** Reverse pivots, pitches soft to TB, and carries out boot fake.	■ The TB's dropstep allows the FB to clear the area. ■ If the BSG scoop is able to block the Nose, the C is free to block upfield on the backside LB. ■ The TE must maintain his base block on the DE to cut off pursuit down the line. ■ The FSG works to get around the TE's block. He is the key blocker in sealing off the inside pursuit of the playside LB or upfield FS. ■ The QB runs the boot fake, which draws the attention of the backside DE.

Toss 48

38

Bill Lewis

Georgia Tech University

Atlanta, Georgia

Atlantic Coast Conference (1A)

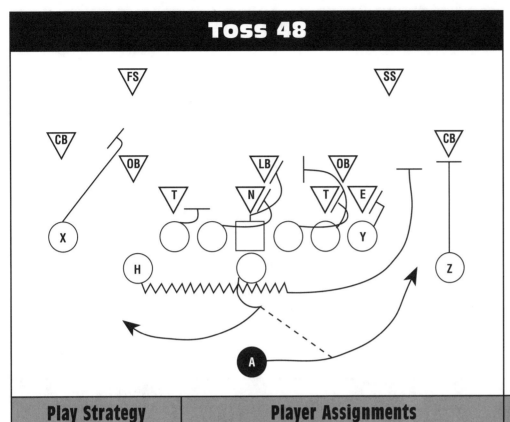

Play Strategy

This is a basic two-back toss sweep that can be run from multiple formations. The play is especially good in short yardage and can be run in any given situation at the TE side or the open side. Coach Lewis can either zone or man block the Toss play from any weak or strong formation.

Player Assignments

Formation: **One-Back**

Offensive Linemen

PST: Blocks wide zone inside with PSG; blocks LB upfield.

PSG: Blocks wide zone playside with PST.

C: Blocks wide zone Nose; blocks LB upfield.

BSG: Blocks wide zone playside Nose with C.

BST: Blocks wide zone playside.

Receivers and Backs

X: Blocks backside cutoff.

Y: Reach blocks outside defender; zone blocks defender inside.

Z: Blocks CB downfield.

H: Motions across, turns upfield past TE, and blocks inside containment.

A: Takes toss and runs parallel 3 steps; reads TE's block.

QB: Reverse pivots, tosses a dead-handed pitch to A, and runs opposite.

Coaching Points

- The TE must maintain block contact with the defender; he prefers to turn inside but takes the defender any direction.

- The H motion (hide to) timing with snap allows the motion back a better angle to block in front of A.

- Another option that can be called is man blocking.

- H blocks #3 at the open side and blocks #4 at the TE side.

- The toss always has H as the lead blocker for A in any alignment.

Jim Walden

Iowa State University

Ames, Iowa

Big Eight Conference
(1A)

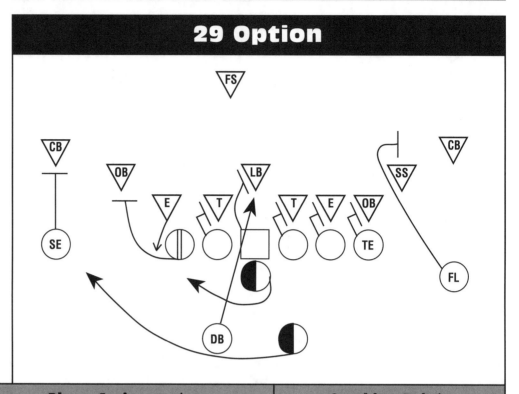

29 Option

Play Strategy

This is the companion play to the counterdive. The theory behind 29 is that defenses cannot stop the dive effectively without being weak outside vs. the option. By running it effectively, defenses are forced to defend the counterdive. This allows them to run the option or vice versa. The counterdive comes first, then the option.

Player Assignments

Formation: **Veer**

Offensive Linemen

ONT: Blocks #2. Never counts end man on LOS as #2. He is optioned.

ONG: Blocks #1, either down linemen or LB.

C: Blocks over, uses playside gap technique, and protects gap.

OFG: Blocks #1, uses playside gap technique, and vs. eagle, blocks man over.

OFT: Blocks #2, uses playside gap technique, and vs. eagle, blocks man over.

Receivers and Backs

SE: Applies rule blocking. Blocks defender over.

TE: Applies rule blocking: onside, arc blocks #4. Offside, blocks #3.

WR: Applies rule blocking: onside and offside. Blocks defender over.

DB: Makes great dive fake with QB using the center guard gap as landmark. Aligns at 4-1/2 yards.

PB: Comes across in pitch relationship, alert for a quick pitch. Keeps pitch relationship with QB.

QB: Reverse pivots, fakes to the DB and options by attacking the EMOL's inside shoulder.

Coaching Points

- Center: blocking technique includes a good scramble. Protects playside gap by aiming at a point inside the hip on the next down lineman up to chop the LB.

- Onside guard: Against down linemen blocks them through the outside breast and gets movement. He drives straight out against the LB and, at the last moment, veers to chop.

- Onside tackle: If #2 is the end man on the LOS, he pulls, gets width, and blocks the first LB from outside-in.

- Onside tight end: when the Offside TE releases inside to cut off the safety, he uses an arc release technique to block #4. He must be alert for two-man rule and roll coverage.

- Wide receiver: if the guard is uncovered, he must be alert for End Out.

- Diveback: hits the hole full speed until 2 yards past LOS. He tries to be tackled. If not, he cut blocks the first man.

- Pitchback: quick steps with the outside foot opposite from the way the play is called.

28 Option

40

Bruce Keith

Sheridan High School

Sheridan, Wyoming

(1972–1993)

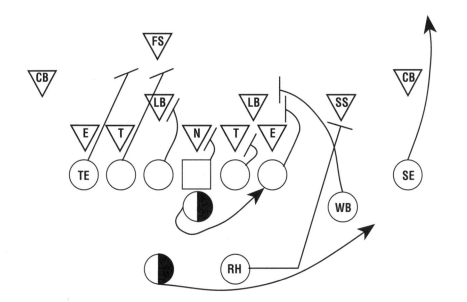

Play Strategy

The decision to use the lead option depends more on what the defense is attacking than on down or distance. When line stunts and LB blitzes are effective in stopping the veer attack, Coach Keith seals off the inside and runs the lead option to the perimeter. Versus aggressive pressure defenses, the lead option can quickly turn into a sweep play. The play is run from multiple formations to both the strong and weak side. Four perimeter blocking schemes are used with the crack calls. Four play action passes may also be called in the lead option series.

Player Assignments

Formation: **Veer**

Offensive Linemen

ONT: Bounce blocks the 5 technique tackle with TE. If 5 technique tackle is the EMOL, releases inside/outside and blocks first LB inside. If man on is not EMOL, blocks base.

ONG: Blocks base. Versus a split front, fold blocks with tackle.

C: If covered, man on blocks; if uncovered, fills for pulling OFG.

OFG: Base blocks or pulls around the OST, blocks defender responsible for filling the alley.

OFT: Base blocks; sprints downfield to block.

Receivers and Backs

TE: If playside, bounce blocks the 5 technique tackle; continues to block LB. If no 5 technique tackle, blocks the first LB inside. If backside, blocks the secondary defender in the middle third.

SE: Blocks base rule on CB or crack call; blocks inside on SS.

WB: Blocks base rule on SS or crack call; blocks inside on LB.

RH: Sprints to point 2 yards wide of EMOL, turns upfield, and blocks the secondary force man.

LH: Sprints laterally; receives pitch immediately.

QB: Reverse pivots; works downhill toward his option key, the EMOL.

Coaching Points

■ If the OFG pulls, the ONG, C, or OFT is responsible for filling the gap.

■ As lead blocker, the RH is aware that the crack call brings the force defender quickly.

■ The QB is taught to attack the inside shoulder of the EMOL for pitch or keep key. The QB must pitch immediately if confronted with a "fire" stunt by the DE.

■ The LH cuts off the block of the lead back.

Ken Hatfield

Rice University

Houston, Texas

Southwest Conference
(1A)

Inside Read Option

Play Strategy	Player Assignments	Coaching Points

Play Strategy

The Inside Read Option is the basic play used in the triple-option series. On any given play, there are three potential runners to carry the ball. Early in the game, the defensive alignments used to stop the option are tested. Blocking rules are applied.

Player Assignments

Formation: **Bone**

Offensive Linemen

OT: Odd call: arc releases; blocks outside zone route to seal OB. Even call: arc releases; blocks inside zone route to drive OB to backside LB. Overload call: blocks inside zone route to drive OB to backside LB.

OG: Odd call: no defender in box; blocks zone route for OB. Even call: defender in box with no PLB; drive blocks defender in box. Overload call: defender in box with PSLB; drive blocks defender in box.

C: Cutoff blocks 0, 1, A. Drive blocks OB to backside LB.

BG and BT: Scoop block playside.

Receivers and Backs

SE: Backside, releases inside to cutoff block CB. Onside, releases to stalk block CB.

FB: Runs track at outside leg of OG, meshes with QB, and fakes or receives the ball.

RH: Lead blocks SS; if called, log blocks OB.

LH: Runs parallel with the QB; maintains a pitch relationship. On pitch, follows RH lead block.

QB: Opens at 45 degrees, reaches deep to FB, safety rides the ball into FB's stomach, and reads the first defensive man outside OG. If defender's near shoulder comes down to take the FB, pulls the ball, and options the next defender out.

Coaching Points

■ QB reads the first defensive man; with any action other than near shoulder down, he gives the ball to the FB.

■ OT hears "brown" or "buster" call from OG and combo blocks with OG. OT must be alert to take stack route vs. a stack defense.

■ If "slip" call, OG combo blocks with C. If "brown" call vs. 3 technique defender, combo blocks with OT. If "brown" call, vs. defender B gap, combo blocks with OT.

■ C is alert for the "slip" call vs. shade 50, vs. 1 to 2 technique defender, and over middle LB.

■ The blocking schemes are designed to handle odd, even, and overload defenses.

■ Box is defined from 1 technique to inside leg of OT (B gap only).

Spread 12

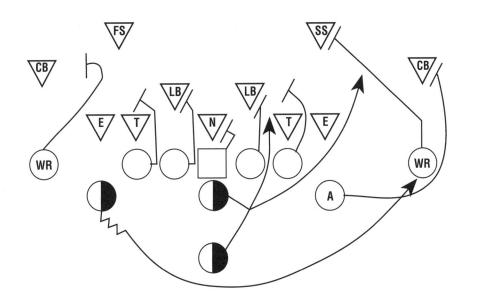

Bob Wagner

University of Hawaii

Honolulu, Hawaii

Western Athletic
Conference (1A)

Play Strategy	Player Assignments	Coaching Points

Play Strategy

This high stakes play can be run on any down or situation. Defensive coordinators know that the triple option upsets most defensive schemes. By adding run-and-shoot passing principles to this same look, additional preparation is required by the opposition. With two wideouts and no TE, the defense is stretched horizontally. The play can be run from Tight Double Slot and Trips.

Player Assignments

Formation: **Double Slot**

Offensive Linemen

BST: Scoop blocks DT to B gap. Cuts off backside pursuit, gets into legs, and executes downfield.

BSG: Scoop blocks A gap to backside LB.

C: Base blocks Nose.

PSG: Base releases to block playside LB to FS. Possibly helps on Nose. Seals perimeter and does not chase.

PST: Base releases to block playside LB to FS. Seals perimeter and does not chase.

Receivers and Backs

BSWR: Blocks FS to backside CB.

BSA: Trails motion with speed; maintains pitch relationship with the QB.

PSWR: Releases; blocks deep defender.

PSA: Dropsteps; blocks force defender.

TB: Runs dive option attack.

QB: Opens and gets ball deep to TB, rides (makes read). Continues down line (reads pitch key). Goes upfield.

Coaching Points

■ This potent offense scores lots of points because special attention is given to executing the triple option.

■ Mental preparation is essential in an effective option attack. While reading the triple, the QB is coached to go with what he believes he sees. There is no second guessing.

■ The BSA is responsible for staying with the QB in a pitch relationship. He expects to receive the pitch.

■ The TB runs dive track with his shoulders square at the LOS. He works to get upfield 5 yards.

■ The PSA's dropstep helps because he cannot cut too soon when the force defender plays soft. When that happens, he stays up to stalk block.

Herb Meyer

El Camino High School

Oceanside, California

Trips Right-Belly Option Right

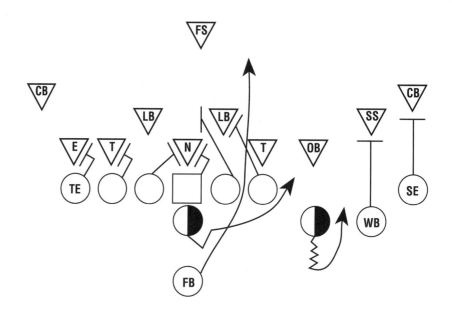

Play Strategy	Player Assignments	Coaching Points

Play Strategy

This play can be called on any down or distance situation. The play is most effective in trips formation when the ball is on the hashmark. When the DT closes hard inside in an attempt to stop the belly give, the second and third phases of the triple option are initiated. Having the SB become the pitchback forces the DE to either close on the QB or stay with the SB.

Player Assignments

Formation: **Trips**

Offensive Linemen

ONT: Splits enough to move DT; blocks down to wall off the inside.

ONG: Blocks down to wall off the inside.

C: Blocks Nose or onside gap.

OFT and OFG: Reach block to cut off inside gap.

Receivers and Backs

TE: Releases inside to block FS.

SE: Alignment is halfway between hashmark and sideline. Releases outside to stalk block CB.

WB: Splits 3 yards outside the hashmark; releases outside to stalk block SS.

FB: Attacks outside leg of ONG; runs the inside veer track.

SB: On snap, backs out 1, 2, 3 while watching the QB for disconnect; swings for possible pitch.

QB: Opens at a 45-degree angle, reaches back with the ball to mesh with the FB off his back foot, and snaps his head around to read the first DL past ONT. He steps at the middle of the ONG while arm-riding the FB. The QB reads the defense to determine which of three options to choose.

Coaching Points

- ONT splits out, which helps create a good running lane for the veer dive.

- FB reads the handoff key. If the DT doesn't attack, he accepts the handoff and turns upfield hard. If the DT attacks, he turns inside, and drives upfield to cutoff block the LB.

- By having the SB read the QB's disconnect with FB, he sets up the correct timing and spacing for the pitch relationship with the QB.

- The QB reads the two unblocked defenders outside the ONT. If the key attacks the FB, the QB withdraws the ball and disconnects with the FB sprinting downfield at the inside leg of the DE. If the DE attacks, the QB pitches to the SB. If not, he keeps the ball upfield.

Wingback Trap Option

Jarrell Williams

Springdale High School

Springdale, Arkansas

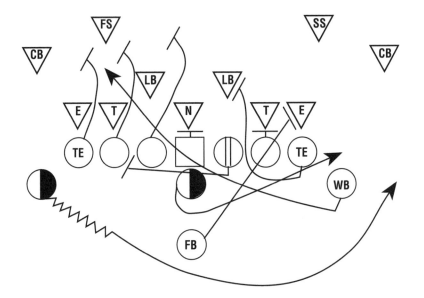

Play Strategy

Coach Williams especially likes to run this play against man coverage because it opens up strongside option routes for the QB and HB. The trap option is set up by running the inside trap. This causes the defense to read WB counteraction. A third dimension, which also helps keep the defense honest, is a play action pass using the same movement and involving the WSE.

Player Assignments

Formation: **Double Wing**

Offensive Linemen

WST: Blocks #2 for 2 counts, then releases downfield to block.

WSG: Blocks #1 for 2 counts, then releases downfield to block.

C: Blocks 0 away from the direction of the play.

SSG: Pulls; turns up into A gap on weak side to block first defender.

SST: Blocks #2 away from the direction of the play.

Receivers and Backs

WSE: Blocks #3 for one count; releases downfield to block.

SSE: Pulls; turns up into A gap on strong side.

FB: Blocks DE over SSE inside out.

HB: Goes in motion behind FB; is the pitch back for the option.

WB: Makes a good fake with the QB on inside trap.

QB: Reverses out and makes handfake to WB; runs option outside.

Coaching Points

■ While going through both A gaps, the pulling SSG and SSE seal off the inside so that the QB can make a good fake.

■ The better the fake between the QB and WB, the more the defense reads run on the weak side.

■ The key block is made by the FB, who works to block the DE inside so that the QB can run free outside.

Part II

Passing Plays

Pass-oriented coaches never die, they just keep studying defenses and designing ways to attack them. Its not that such coaches are better strategists than their run-oriented counterparts, it's just that they have more weapons in their arsenal. And so they construct their elaborate play lists, à la Bill Walsh, throw the ball 30+ times, and make you outscore them.

Coaches who face the teams of Steve Spurrier at Florida, Keith Gilbertson at University of California, or LaVell Edwards at Brigham Young, know the score. Their offense has to put up some big numbers. And their defense had better be ready for a long game.

These are controlled passing schemes, centered on precise timing and pinpoint accuracy. A proficient quarterback is a must. So is good blocking, although most coaches design "hot" and "sight" adjustment reads that allow the quarterback to dump the ball off. No matter what innovations coaches might add, however, the old maxim applies: If you can protect the quarterback and throw with accuracy, you're sure to have the defense screaming for mercy. The passing game also relies on intelligent, spontaneous play. Quarterbacks must make quick pre- and postsnap reads, which translate into correct, split-second decisions and flawless execution. Moving the college hashmarks toward the middle of the field has influenced directional pass calls. Who said that quarterbacks get too much attention?

Some offensive passing schemes also require receivers and blockers to read the defense. In the player assignments for plays in this section you'll see what reads are required. For you run-first coaches, there's a variety of play action passes that you're sure to like. These plays are often only as successful as the play from which they were developed. A coach knows that faking a run can create open areas to pass. When both are working, the defense is helpless.

Then there are those of you who can't resist the urge to go DEEP several times a game. Straight drop by the QB and launch. Throw caution—and the pigskin—to the wind. You too should be pleased with the selection of plays that follows. Bombs away!

Play List

Coach	Play	Formation
Play Action Passes		
Keith Gilbertson	224 Z Dig	I
Ron Schipper	Right I Pro 23 Cross Boot	I
Glen Mason	417 Kansas	I
Steve Spurrier	I-Right Sprint Draw 4 Pass X Option	I
Rich Brooks	Crack Screen Left	I
Mike Huard	Boot Right	I
Tom Marcucci	Cross Buck Pass	I
Al Fracassa	I-Right Counter Pass Right	I
Joe Kinnan	Trap Option Pass	I
Rich Zinanni	Counter 23 Pass	I
Wally Sheets	Play Pass 33-37 Double Cross	I
Freddie James	Pro Set Right 77 Pass	I
Gary Moeller	470 Scan	I
Jim Nagel	956 Waggle Pass	Double Slot
Tony Severino	58 Pass 911 X	Wing-T
Jim Sauls	20 Waggle	Wing-T
Walt Braun	48 Pass	Wing-T
Jimmie Keeling	96	One-Back
Jim Wacker	Pro Right 32 Naked	One-Back
Joe Petricca	Ace Right Jet Strong Z F	One-Back
Dave Roberts	Left 5 Naked Pitch	One-Back
Lou Tepper	Slot Shovel Right	One-Back
Terry Allen	528	Split Backs
Joe Miller	49 Rail	Split Backs
Frosty Westering	Flackin Right	Split Backs Strong
Bill Mallory	80 X-Out	Pro
Dropback Passes		
Spike Dykes	71 B Option	I
Dick Dullaghan	49 Tailback Screen	I

Coach	Play	Formation
Dennis Erickson	Doubles Left 71X	One-Back
Jim Donnan	Doubles Right 168 Shallow/Wide	One-Back
Tom Grippa	82 Up	One-Back
Jerry Schliem	40 Y/A Option	One-Back
Jack Stark	Dubs Right 93X-Divide	One-Back
Alan Paturzo	Spread Right Rip 60 Go	One-Back
Steve Axman	Left Cat Bunch 247 Pivot	One-Back
John Mackovic	Red Right 86 X Post	Split Backs
LaVell Edwards	Split Right 958	Split Backs
Tom Coughlin	74-75 Double Seam	Split Backs
Jim Caldwell	52 Stop	Split Backs
Bruce Snyder	Brown 538 Angle	Split Backs
Jack Johnson	Check Pass	Split Backs
Harry Welch	Z Burst	Split Backs
Bob McQueen	Trey Left Fan Right 94 Y Choice	Trips
Don Read	20 Read	Double Slot
Jeff Scurran	Gangster Pass Right: Curl & Out	Double Slot

Keith Gilbertson

University of California

Berkeley, California

Pac-10 Conference (1A)

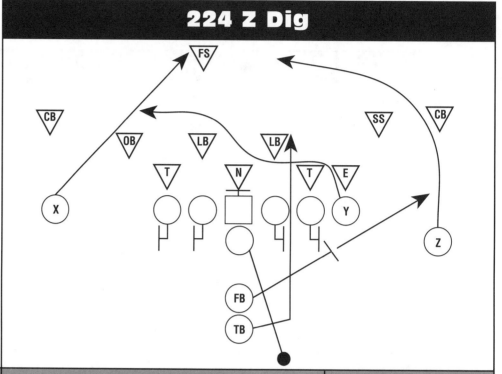

224 Z Dig

Play Strategy	Player Assignments	Coaching Points

Play Strategy

To avoid the nickel defense, Coach Gilbertson especially likes to use this play on first and second down. When in the red zone, the post corner route can be added for X, Y, or Z. The bomber formation, which features three receivers and two backs, adds another wrinkle to the play.

Player Assignments

Formation: **I-Formation**

Offensive Linemen

ST: Blocks strongside B gap. Sell run.

SG: Blocks strongside A gap. Sell run.

C: If covered, "me and you" call with SG. If uncovered, blocks middle to backside LB.

WG: Blocks weakside B gap.

WT: Blocks widest rusher.

Receivers and Backs

X: Runs a 16-yard post dig route.

Z: Takes shorter split; runs a post route.

Y: Releases inside; runs drag route.

FB: Checks force defender or first man outside ST; releases to flat route.

TB: Fakes 24 roll, keys frontside inside LB, and releases on checkdown route.

QB: Opens to TB, fakes TB, gets depth, and sets up at 8 to 9 yards.

Coaching Points

■ If "F flat" is called, the FB is the "hot" receiver. He quickly looks for the ball.

■ The TB fakes over the ball and blocks the play-side inside LB. The TB must be alert for the L and R call and must block the next LB over to the called side.

■ One of the trademarks of the play is for the receivers to separate from their defenders. Versus man coverage, the QB looks for X or Y to be running away from their defenders.

■ The QB looks first to Z on the post route. Versus zone, he looks for X in a window. If X is not open, he lays the ball off to Y or the TB/FB.

Right I Pro 23 Cross Boot

Ron Schipper

Central College

Pella, Iowa

Iowa Conference
(NCAA III)

Play Strategy

The Cross Boot is an outstanding first-down play and, after running inside successfully, is also used for short-yardage third-down calls. You can use this play almost anywhere on the field. It provides an excellent deep pass threat to both the frontside flag route and the backside post route. Like most play action passes, this play should follow the use of companion plays, the FB Trap and TB Cross. The crossing action of the backs freezes both LBs and the FS.

Player Assignments

Formation: I-Formation

Offensive Linemen

RT: If covered, blocks man; if uncovered, steps to B gap and checks QB's backside. If QB is not being chased, stays solid.

RG: If covered, blocks man; if uncovered, pulls right and blocks first man outside the OT.

C: If covered, blocks man; if uncovered, blocks backside A gap.

LG: Pulls right parallel to LOS for 2 steps, then goes 4 yards deep. Becomes personal protector for the QB.

LT: If covered, blocks man; if uncovered, steps to B. If no one comes, hinges.

Receivers and Backs

TE: Slams for 2 counts; releases into flat at a depth of 8 to 10 yards.

SE: Drives at CB; releases on deep route on seam behind the FS.

WB: Drives hard at SS; breaks on deep flag route.

FB: Drives to inside leg of RG, attacks LB, and releases right to open spot.

TB: Fakes 23 cross and picks up the most dangerous defender coming his way. Checks backside A and B gaps; checks the outside rush man.

QB: Opens right, fakes 23 cross, and then boots right.

Coaching Points

■ To achieve the effectiveness of play action, all must carry out their assignments like it is going to be a run.

■ Both the TB and FB attack the LOS.

■ The TB checks the area vacated by the pulling LG before blocking the outside rush.

■ Whether it's an odd or even defense determines the path the FB uses to get into the face of the LB. Only then can he release to the open spot.

■ The QB's first step must give the FB room to attack the LB. He must not hurry the TB fake.

■ The QB is coached to get sufficient depth so that he can get shoulders turned upfield and be in a position to throw. He targets the SE, who is breaking on a deep post route in the seam.

■ It is very important for the TE to aggressively slam block the man on him for 2 counts before releasing to the flat. This helps to avoid quick outside pressure.

47

Glen Mason

University of Kansas

Lawrence, Kansas

Big Eight Conference
(1A)

417 Kansas

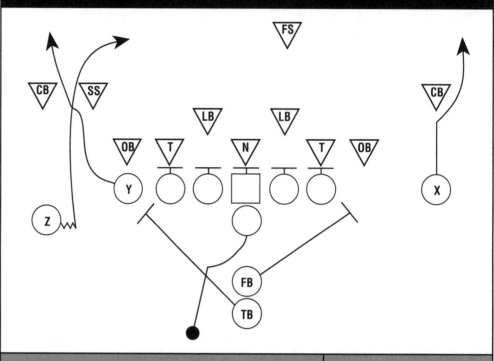

Play Strategy

Call this play on first down and 10, second down and medium, or third down, medium to short. Coach Mason refers to the play as the "run down pass." His strategy is to run the onside zone play into the boundary with the wing or motion man as an extra blocker. When the CB or safeties start to play run support, it's a good time to run this play action pass. The play can be run from the I-Wing with motion to wing or from the Spread-Wing with motion to wing.

Player Assignments

Formation: **I-Formation**

Offensive Linemen

ONT: Blocks man over or outside.

ONG: Blocks man over or inside.

C: Blocks man over or offside.

OFG: Blocks man over or inside-out.

OFT: Blocks man over or inside-out.

Receivers and Backs

X: Runs an out-and-up route at depth of 12 yards.

Y: Releases vertical; runs wheel route.

Z: Runs upfield at depth of 12 yards; breaks post route.

FB: Blocks first LB outside-in on backside.

TB: Fakes 17; blocks first LB outside-in playside.

QB: Fakes 17 with TB, drops eyes into pocket after fake, and runs straight back at depth of 9 to 10 yards. Reads CB on called side. If CB plays run, throws quickly to Y. If CB plays Z, throws to outside shoulder of Y and runs fade route into the numbers.

Coaching Points

■ The line must sell run by coming off the ball with a low-tucked butt. It uses high-pressure control to maintain blocks.

■ Since the ball may be thrown late to X, the route is run slowly.

■ Z must not cross the near upright when running the post route.

■ After turning upfield, Y times his route to go behind post route by Z.

■ The TB and QB must sell the run fake. After faking, the TB must be alert for quick pressure from playside.

■ After going deep away from the LOS, the QB quickly turns his eyes around to read the called side CB.

I-Right Sprint Draw 4 Pass X Option

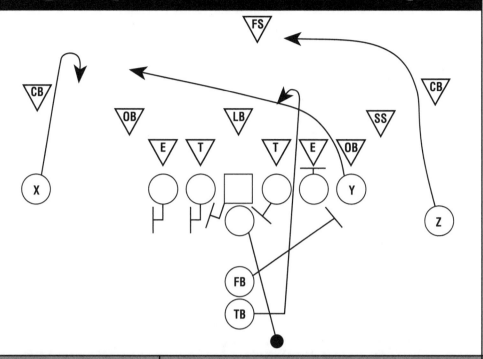

Steve Spurrier

University of Florida

Gainesville, Florida

Southeastern
Conference (1A)

Play Strategy

Coach Spurrier runs this play action pass after establishing the sprint draw run. It is run on any given down and is not always run in pass situations. The X-Option is very effective when X is on the short side.

Player Assignments

Formation: **I-Formation**

Offensive Linemen

These blocking rules are for the Sprint Draw protection package.

ST: Blocks #2.

SG: Blocks backside gap.

C: Blocks backside gap.

WG: Blocks backside gap.

WT: Blocks backside gap.

Receivers and Backs

X: If CB plays off, runs a 16-yard curl route; if CB plays bump and run or cover 2 zone, runs a corner route.

Z: Runs across the middle about 17 to 18 yards deep or runs a short post route.

Y: Releases inside; runs an 8-yard drag route to X-side.

FB: Blocks playside EMOL.

TB: Executes a good fake, hooks up at depth of 5 to 6 yards between SG and ST.

QB: Fronts out, fakes TB sprint draw, sets up, has choice to throw to X running curl route or corner route or Y running drag route. If neither is open, throws to TB hook route in middle.

Coaching Points

- Both backs are involved in the Sprint Draw 4 pass protection package. After faking the draw, the FB checks the outside blitz. The TB must be prepared to block inside the LB blitz.

- QB takes 7 steps and gives a short fake to the TB before setting up to throw.

- Z runs up the hash-mark before breaking across or running the short post route.

- If the QB finds no receivers open, he is taught to throw the ball away or to run for a touchdown.

Rich Brooks

University of Oregon

Eugene, Oregon

Pac-10 Conference (1A)

Crack Screen Left

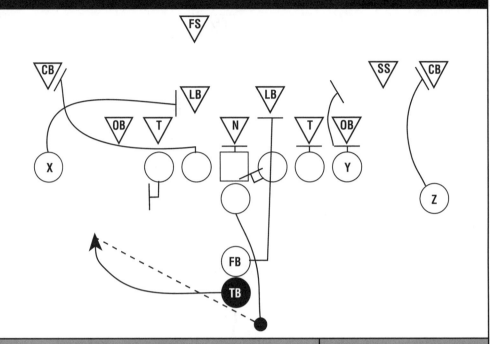

Play Strategy	Player Assignments	Coaching Points

Play Strategy

The decision to use this play depends more on what the defense is showing than down and distance. The Crack Screen works effectively with the inside draw play. After faking the draw, the screen away will be called against any weakside pressure. Using different calls, the line can block defensive fronts like 50 (odd), 50 shade reducer (odd), 20 (stack), 80 (split), 53 (odd), 53 flop (odd), or bear.

Player Assignments

Formation: **I-Formation**

Offensive Linemen

ONT: Blocks on or outside.

ONG: Releases flat; kicks out defender in flat. If covered, slams defender inside while releasing.

C: Blocks onside area; looks downfield to block Will LB.

OFT: Blocks on, over, or downfield.

OFG: Blocks on, over, or downfield.

Receivers and Backs

X: Crack blocks on Liz LB to next level. In twin, blocks #2.

Y: Rocks downfield.

Z: Runs inside release to block CB.

FB: Fakes draw; blocks Mike LB.

TB: Uses jab step; runs flare between crack block and kickout block.

QB: Runs a 5-step drop, fakes FB Draw, and throws to TB.

Coaching Points

- ONT must be alert for the "bingo" call to turnout on DE; OFT and OFG must be alert for the "3 solo" call to block the defender over OFT.

- The C must be alert for the "base" call to stay and block Nose.

- The TB does not take a jab step when in I-formation. When throwing to the TB, the QB may back pedal if Liz LB is a threat.

- The QB audibles to "cut" when facing a nickel, Liz LB, or press.

- SE does not block defender in press situation.

Boot Right

Mike Huard

Puyallup High School
Puyallup, Washington

Play Strategy	Player Assignments	Coaching Points

Play Strategy

Coach Huard prefers to use this play action pass when the defense is thinking run, such as on a second or third down and short. The SE route is altered to a corner route inside the +25-yard line. If defenders are honoring the *go* route, the SE will adjust to an 18-yard comeback route. On-field adjustments are built into this play, which can be run out of all one-back or two-back sets.

Player Assignments

Formation: **I-Formation**

Offensive Linemen

PST: Aggressively blocks inside gap.

PSG: Aggressively blocks man inside gap.

C: If covered, blocks BSG gap with help from PSG. If uncovered, blocks BSG gap.

BSG: Pulls playside to block EMOL.

BST: Blocks down to inside gap.

Receivers and Backs

TE: Releases inside, runs behind LBs to a depth of 12 yards, and mirrors the width of QB.

SE: Runs deep go route to clear deep 1/3 or 1/2 coverages.

FL: Runs a deep clear route between CB and SS.

FB: Releases outside DE in flat route 2 to 5 yards deep.

TB: Carries out fake as long as possible; blocks first defender outside BST.

QB: Opens playside, handfakes to TB on third step, pauses a half-second, and at depth of 9 yards sets up behind PST.

Coaching Points

- Gap protection requires the line to spend extra time picking up inside LB stunts.

- It is important that the line blocks aggressively on the LOS and knows that the QB launch point is behind the PST or, if contain is blocked, the QB goes outside.

- The BSG pulls shallow behind C, then arches to a 4-yard depth behind the PST. He kickout blocks or seals containment.

- With shoulders square, the TE finds a window vs. zone; vs. man, he runs away.

- Width is more important than depth when the FB runs the flat route. The FB slam blocks against OB or SS stunt before releasing into flat. In TE alignment, he blocks 2 counts before running into flat.

- After cross-over-plant steps, the TB fakes into the LOS with speed.

- With his back to the defense, the QB pivots at 6 o'clock, open-hand fakes to the TB, pauses for timing, and helps sell the TB fake inside. If contain is blocked, the QB rolls out toward the LOS, leaving the launch point. Versus outside pressure, the QB looks immediately for the FB; vs. the zone, he throws off the flat defender to the TE. Another outlet for the QB is to run upfield or pass a throwaway. Against a double blitz at LOS, the QB can check out of this play.

51

Tom Marcucci

Notre Dame High School

West Haven, Connecticut

Cross Buck Pass

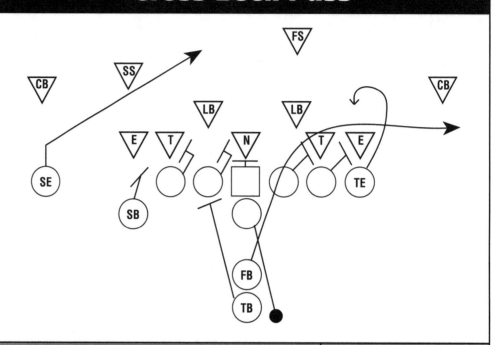

Play Strategy

Coach Marcucci likes to run the play on first down or second and short. It is best run into the short side or away from the SS. The play can be run in any formation from a slot or tight side. Complementary plays, buck and crossbuck, help to set up this play action pass.

Player Assignments

Formation: **I-Formation**

Offensive Linemen

FST: Fan protection, blocks out DT.

FSG: Fan protection, blocks out DE.

C: Blocks Nose, playside gap.

BSG: Aggressively cup blocks playside.

BST: Aggressively cup blocks playside.

Receivers and Backs

SE: Runs backside post route or dig route.

TE: Releases free; runs curl route away from the LB.

SB: Aggressively cup blocks backside.

FB: Fakes buck over FSG; releases into the flat. If he stunts, blocks LB.

TB: Fakes crossbuck over BSG; blocks first defender to show.

QB: Flash fakes FB and TB, drops back, and looks to throw to FB in flat.

Coaching Points

■ Basic protection is to aggressively block fan on playside (TE side) and aggressively cup block on the slot side.

■ If frontside LB fills or stunts, the FB must block him. The TE becomes the primary receiver.

■ The QB's read is the frontside LB. If the LB goes to the flat, the QB throws to TE. If the LB stays with the curl, the QB throws to FB.

■ The flash fake to the FB does not have to be good, but the TB's fake has to be a good one.

■ This is an excellent play for a pass-catching FB.

■ If not needed in protection, the TB will spot up as an outlet for the QB.

I-Right Counter Pass Right

Al Fracassa

Brother Rice High School

Birmingham, Michigan

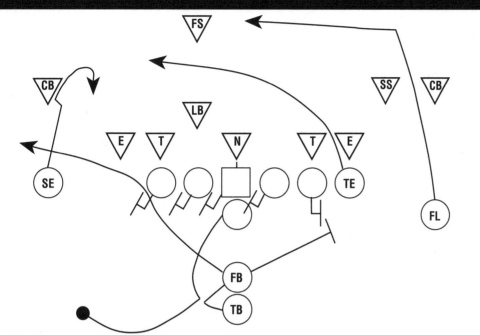

Play Strategy	Player Assignments	Coaching Points

Play Strategy

You can use this play in either direction on first down and short yardage. A good time to run this play action pass is after running the counterplay off-tackle. When the pass is thrown to the short boundary side, the percentage of completions has been very high. The play is also run from a one-back set with slot to the split side or with split backs (i.e., the FB behind the QB and the I-Back behind the LT).

Player Assignments

Formation: **I-Formation**

Offensive Linemen

LT: Zone blocks; is responsible for area outside. Looks for DE.

LG: Zone blocks; is responsible for LT area.

C: Zone blocks; is responsible for LG area.

RG: Zone blocks; is responsible for C area. Looks for slanting Nose.

RT: Zone blocks; is responsible for RG area. If no defender shows, hinge blocks.

Receivers and Backs

SE: Runs upfield hard for 7 yards, fakes corner route, runs post route to 15 yards, and curls back to 8 yards.

TE: Runs upfield 4 to 5 yards; works across deep to corner behind the SE curl.

FL: Runs upfield 8 yards, breaks post route for 8 yards, and digs hard across at 16 yards.

FB: Checks first defender outside LT; slips into flat at depth of 4 to 5 yards.

TB: Takes short left step, takes right crossover, takes another left jab step, and runs counter-fake with the QB to seal off backside DE.

QB: Opens left, sprints deep for fake handoff to I-Back, gains depth after fake, and starts progressive read of receivers.

Coaching Points

■ The SE adjusts curl route to an open spot away from the LB and drops behind while the TE is running the corner route. The FL adjusts his crossing speed to get into an open area.

■ While running the flat route, the FB, as primary receiver, looks quickly for the ball.

■ The I-Back makes a good counter-fake with the QB and tries to convince the defense that he has the ball. In sealing the backside, he first blocks any defender that shows or helps block the inside. In Split Backs Formation, the I-Back must go behind the FB when he fakes the counterplay.

■ The QB's progressive reads are as follows: (1) The #1 receiver is the FB in the flat. If open, the ball is thrown immediately. (2) The #2 receiver is the SE running the curl route. (3) The #3 receiver is the TE in the corner. (4) The #4 receiver is the FL crossing deep. At times, Coach Fracassa changes the progressive order for the QB.

■ As soon as he finishes the I-Back fake, the QB eyes the receivers, sprints hard, squares his shoulders, and hits the open receiver.

Joe Kinnan

Manatee High School

Bradenton, Florida

Trap Option Pass

Play Strategy

This play runs better after establishing the trap option, in which the DBs show run support. If the three receivers sell the run, they can get open for the pass. Down and distance are not as important as how the defense reacts to the run. Coach Kinnan takes advantage of overaggressive DBs.

Player Assignments

Formation: **I-Formation**

Offensive Linemen

PST: If covered, blocks man on. If not, blocks gap.

PSG: If covered, blocks man on. If not, blocks gap.

C: Blocks gap for the pulling BSG.

BSG: Pulls and blocks the playside DE area.

BST: Blocks the backside DE area.

Receivers and Backs

WR: Both wide receivers run 8-yard stop routes.

FB: Steps with his playside foot, aims for the middle of C, and fakes a run to daylight while looking to block the playside LB.

TB: Freezes until the QB has taken his second step. Sprints to a point on the LOS, which is 10 yards outside the PST's alignment.

QB: Opens to playside, clears the midline, and fakes the ball to the FB. Continues 3 steps parallel to the LOS; throws to first open receiver from the inside out. If all receivers are covered, pitches the ball to the TB.

SB: Splits the distance between the PST and the SE; runs an 8-yard stop route.

Coaching Points

■ Line calls are necessary. The PST gives the call if blocking gap, the PSG gives the call if covered and blocking inside, and C gives the call if the pulling BSG and C are both covered. The BST blocks zone if the BSG is covered.

■ All three potential receivers establish eye contact with the DB over them and show their hands as if blocking for a run.

■ If all receivers are covered, the TB must be alert to receive the pitch from the QB. He is coached to look the ball into his hands.

■ The first open receiver is the correct target for the QB's throw. The pitch to the TB is the last choice.

Counter 23 Pass

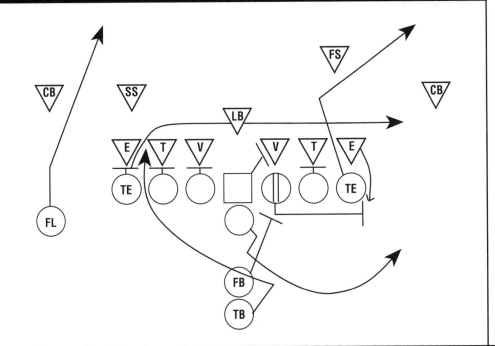

Rich Zinanni

Bishop McNamara High School

Kankakee, Illinois

Play Strategy	Player Assignments	Coaching Points

Play Strategy

Coach Zinanni likes the Counter 23 Pass in short-yardage situations. The play can be set up by the FB dive and the TB counter. If the QB can't turn the corner, he can pull up and throw deep or short. Power I set is used in short yardage situations with HB blocking DE, guard stays.

Player Assignments

Formation: **I-Formation**

Offensive Linemen

ONT: Aggressively blocks man on.

ONG: Pulls playside; log blocks the DE.

C: If covered, blocks man on. If uncovered, blocks playside gap.

LG: If covered, blocks man on. If uncovered, blocks playside gap.

LT: Aggressively blocks man on.

Receivers and Backs

RE: Releases inside, runs toward the FS, breaks off, and runs corner route.

LE: Releases inside; runs drag route across the field into playside flat.

FL: Runs upfield at the FS.

FB: Aims at the RG, receives fake, and blocks any defender to show.

TB: Steps toward RT, receives counterfake, and runs at outside shoulder of LT.

QB: Steps playside, fakes to FB, fakes to TB, runs playside bootleg, and attacks the corner.

Coaching Points

■ Linemen should block aggressively so that the defense reads run.

■ A key for the pulling guard is to get depth and be in a position to log block the DE. The ONG does not pull if the formation is a Power I.

■ Two important fakes are key to the execution of the play. The QB first makes a poor fake to the FB and then makes a great fake to the TB.

■ After the TB fake, the QB attacks the corner with an option to run or pass.

Wally Sheets

Washington High School

Cedar Rapids, Iowa

Play Pass 33-37 Double Cross

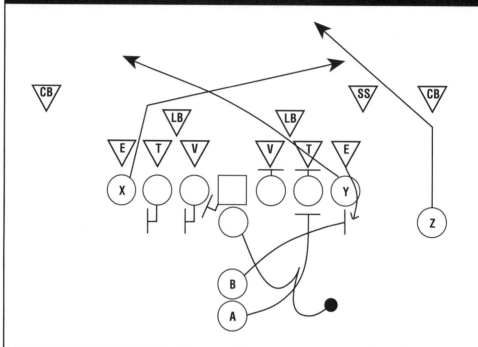

Play Strategy	Player Assignments	Coaching Points
The defense can expect Coach Sheets to call this play inside the 10-yard line. This pass may also be used as a 2-point conversion play. This double tight formation requires the defense to be balanced and usually calls for man coverage. The routes remain the same against zone coverage.	Formation: **I-Formation** **Offensive Linemen** **PST:** Base blocks man on; if uncovered, blocks C gap. **PSG:** Base blocks man on; if uncovered, blocks B gap. **C:** Turn blocks at 45 degrees; takes the first man to cross face. **BSG:** Executes a turn block **BST:** Executes a turn block. **Receivers and Backs** **X:** Releases off the ball, runs a crossing pattern, and gains width and depth. **Y:** Releases off the ball, runs a crossing pattern, and gains width and depth underneath X's pattern. **Z:** Runs post pattern, hooks up under the goal post, and works to get open. **B:** Runs kickout block on the first defender outside the PST. **A:** Runs hard to butt of the PST, takes fake from the QB, and blocks the nearest defender. **QB:** Fronts out to ride the belly fake with TB; steps back inside the FB's kickout block to pass.	■ When ready to pass, the QB looks away before throwing to Y, his primary receiver. ■ X must look for the ball any time the QB is under pressure. ■ Due to the double cross patterns, this play is most effective from the double tight formation. ■ The fake between the QB and TB is critical. ■ Y, the primary receiver, must run underneath to avoid a collision with the crossing pattern of X. ■ A reads PST; if covered, blocks B gap; if uncovered, blocks C gap. No one to block, releases to 6 yards.

Pro Set Right 77 Pass

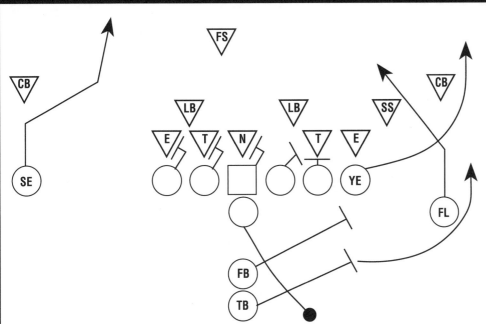

Freddie James

David W. Carter High School

Dallas, Texas

Play Strategy

In his multioffense, Coach James uses speed and deception to mix the pass with the run. Pass 77 is a good example of the kind of play that can be run on any down. The play is used when secondary defenders come to stop the run pounding off-tackle. In this attack, the play may be run from many different formations.

Player Assignments

Formation: **I-Formation**

Offensive Linemen

RT: Blocks gap, on, or over.

RG: Blocks gap, on, or over. If uncovered, blocks playside gap.

C: Blocks Nose, playside gap, or over.

LG: Blocks gap, on, or over.

LT: Blocks gap, on, or over.

Receivers and Backs

SE: Releases upfield; runs post route and up toward FS.

TE: Flexed position, runs flat route at CB and runs upfield.

FL: Releases upfield; runs short post route inside SS.

FB: Blocks playside DE.

TB: Blocks playside; runs swing pass behind the LOS.

QB: Sprints out playside, reads the CB, throws to TE running upfield, or throws to FL on short post route. If not open, throws to TB on swing route.

Coaching Points

■ It is important that both backs stay to block any playside pressure so the QB can stay on his tract. The TB runs his swing route if possible.

■ The crossing pattern is easy for the QB to read to see if the defense is playing man or zone.

■ Pressure from the backside is handled by the LT and LG. C helps to playside.

■ By flexing, the TE has a better change to run his route and not be detained.

■ The QB is taught the 3-step drop technique. If the playside routes are not open, the QB can set his feet and throw to the SE running the post route.

57

470 Scan

Gary Moeller

University of Michigan

Ann Arbor, Michigan

Big Ten Conference (1A)

Play Strategy	Player Assignments	Coaching Points

Play Strategy

After establishing the 24 run, Coach Moeller likes to call this play action pass. The play is called on 1st and 10 or 2nd and medium situations. The play has been successful on any down, especially when the defense is set up to stop the inside run.

Player Assignments

Formation: **I-Formation**

Offensive Linemen

LT: Blocks down, man over.

LG: Blocks first down defender; blocks head up to inside.

C: Blocks backside A gap.

RG: Blocks backside B gap.

RT: Blocks backside C gap.

Receivers and Backs

X: Runs a post corner route, breaks post at 12 yards, and breaks corner at 15 yards.

Z: Runs a seam/hook route. Versus 3 deep, hooks at 15 yards; vs. 2 deep, stays on seam route.

Y: Runs a flag route; breaks at depth of 13 to 14 yards.

FB: Blocks frontside EMOL.

TB: Checks for weakside blitz, runs upfield, and breaks into flat route.

QB: Presnap, checks alignment keys from FS to weakside LB; reads man or zone coverage. Fakes 24 run, takes adjustable 7-step drop, reads strongside progression X, Z, and H.

Coaching Points

- The philosophy of the play is an adjustable 7-step play action pass. The pass comes off the fake of the 24 run play.

- The play is designed to attack all coverages to the strong side and in the intermediate zones.

- The key FB's block on the EMOL allows the QB time to fake, drop, and throw.

- The QB checks his alignment keys, FS or weakside LB and for man or zone coverage. He reads the strongside progression. The QB's faking technique is vital to holding the inside LBs in check.

956 Waggle Pass

Jim Nagel

Ashland High School
Ashland, Oregon

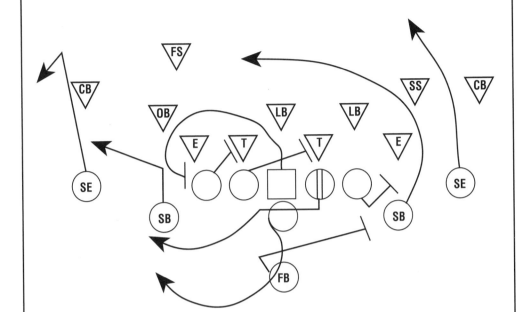

Play Strategy	Player Assignments	Coaching Points

Play Strategy

This play is designed to complement the scissors play (countertrey). The play action pass is called when the backside DE closes hard behind the pulling tackle. The play is run back to the weak side against teams that overload on the trips side. On the goal line, QB checks PSS first and then the drag route, which puts extreme pressure on coverage.

Player Assignments

Formation: **Double Slot**

Offensive Linemen

PST: Fills to onside A gap.

PSG: Pulls; trap blocks to offside A gap.

C: Slides to onside C gap; walls off first defender to show.

BSG: Pulls deep onside; either log blocks or kickout blocks first defender outside PST.

BST: Blocks gap, on, or hinge.

Receivers and Backs

PSR: Runs deep comeback route at a depth of 18 to 20 yards.

BSR: Runs post route.

PSS: Fakes block for 2 counts; runs flat route.

BSS: Runs deep drag route at a depth of 12 to 15 yards.

FB: Fakes 56 scissors; blocks offside.

QB: Slow fakes scissors, gets 7 to 8 yards depth, and forces the corner with run/pass option.

Coaching Points

■ It is important that the PST makes his first step appear the same as if he is pulling for the scissors run play. With a defender on inside shade, he blocks him. While pulling, he blocks the first defender to show on the way to the onside A gap. If the PSG makes BS call, the PST blocks the B gap.

■ The PSG takes a dropstep, works into the LOS, and trap blocks the first defender on his way to the offside A gap. Versus the gap defender, he makes the BS call and blocks the gap defender.

■ The PSG cleans off the Nose first.

■ After faking a block on the goal line, the PSS is often the best receiver to get open on the sideline.

■ If the PSG makes BS call, the C blocks backside. The C's path should be a replacement of the defensive line stances, moving behind the defender and setting up just outside the PST. By working back inside, the C is able to wall off the pursuit. If the QB gives the go call, the C turns upfield to lead block.

Tony Severino

Rockhurst High School

Kansas City, Missouri

58 Pass 911 X

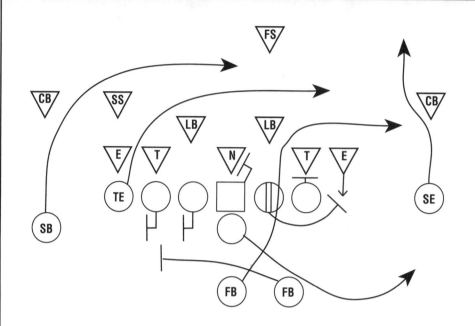

Play Strategy	Player Assignments	Coaching Points

Play Strategy

You can call this play on any down and distance. If the defense is playing cover 3, the play will be called. Depending on the defensive front, either or both guards may pull, which makes it look like a running play. Play success depends on the ability of the QB to get to the corner, reading receivers from outside in.

Player Assignments

Formation: **Wing-T**

Offensive Linemen

RT: Blocks base.

RG: Pulls playside; hook blocks the most danger-ous defender on LOS.

C: Blocks playside for pulling guard.

LG: Hinge blocks backside.

LT: Hinge blocks backside.

Receivers and Backs

SE: Runs 9 route (streak).

TE: Runs 1 route (drag).

SB: Runs upfield 10 yards; flattens playside at 15 yards.

FB: Aiming point is outside RG to open. Flash fakes, avoids contact, and runs in flat.

TB: Counterfakes after counterstep; blocks first backside defender to show.

QB: Flash fakes to the FB to open, ball fakes to TB, and sprints to corner.

Coaching Points

■ The pulling RG is drilled to handle all different kinds of containment. It is vital to get the QB to the corner.

■ The SB and TE's crossing routes and the FB's route in the flat are timed so that each keeps within 5 yards of each other.

■ The QB makes a poor flash fake to the FB. He must not hurry while making a good fake to the TB.

■ After faking, the TB must protect the QB from backside pressure, especially by the DE.

20 Waggle

60

Jim Sauls

Leon High School
Tallahassee, Florida

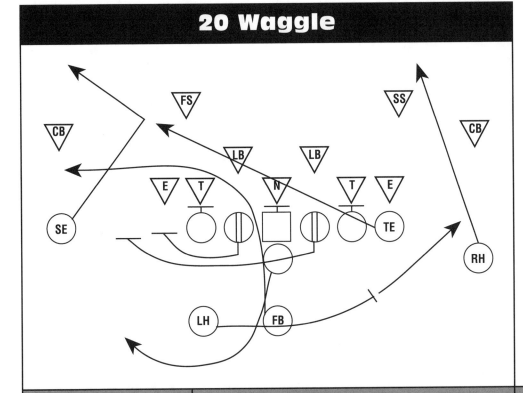

Play Strategy	Player Assignments	Coaching Points

Play Strategy

This play is often run on first down. When planning his strategy for the 20 Waggle, Coach Sauls wants the defense to first respect the 20 Sweep. This misdirectional play is best when defenses overreact to the buck sweep. Also, the play may be run in the spread or slot formations.

Player Assignments

Formation: **Wing-T**

Offensive Linemen

RT: Blocks gap, LB, on, or away.

RG: Pulls left; cleans up any defender that shows.

C: Blocks man on or fills for pulling RG.

LG: Pulls; blocks first man outside LT.

LT: Blocks gap, down or man on.

Receivers and Backs

TE: Runs a crossing pattern at a depth of 15 yards.

SE: Runs inside toward the FS; runs a deep flag route.

RH: In a flanker alignment, runs go route, keys FS.

LH: Fakes 20 Sweep, prepares to block backside DE, or runs the throwback route.

FB: Fakes dive; aims for the inside foot of LG. Slide delays into left flat as receiver.

QB: Reverses pivots, fakes 20 Sweep, and options left to pass or run.

Coaching Points

■ Both guards pull opposite 20 Sweep to block for the QB, who has the option to pass or run.

■ The timing between the FB and the pulling LG is given extra attention.

■ After faking sweep, the QB must get depth when threatening outside. The QB has six options on this plaY: (a) throw to the SE on flag route, (b) throw to the FB in left flat, (c) throw to the TE on a crossing route, (d) throw to the RH on a deep post route behind the FS, (e) pull up and throw to the LH, or (f) keep the ball and run.

Walt Braun

Marysville High School

Marysville, Michigan

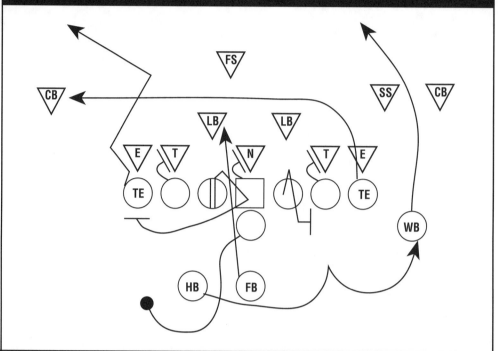

48 Pass

Play Strategy

The bootleg pass is called when a defense reacts to stop the inside dive and off-tackle hole plays. Down and distance are not the key factors in determining this play call. To be successful, the crossbuck series should be established. A change-up route calls for the SE to run a post corner. This play works best when the defense is expecting a run.

Player Assignments

Formation: **Wing-T**

Offensive Linemen

ST: Blocks gap, on, out, or tailgate.

SG: Shows false pull, pivots, and blocks DE.

C: Blocks quickside gap, on, strongside gap, or tailgate.

QG: Blocks gap, on, out, or tailgate.

OT: Blocks out, on, gap, or tailgate.

Receivers and Backs

SE: Aligns inside; runs a corner route.

TE: Releases inside; runs a drag route at a depth of 5 yards.

WB: Runs a deep post route.

FB: Runs at SG/C gap, fakes dive, and works to be tackled by LB.

HB: Fakes quickside off-tackle hole; works to be tackled.

QB: Opens to fake FB dive, steps back to fake HB, puts ball on hip, and runs the bootleg.

Coaching Points

■ The SE is encouraged to deceive the CB by throttling down as if to block; he runs the corner route instead.

■ The timing of the pulling SG and faking of the FB are essential. The SG goes behind and blocks the DE.

■ The QB makes two great fakes to deceive the defense into believing that the play is a run.

■ While running the bootleg, the QB's progressive reads include the SE corner route, the TE drag route, and the FL post route. The QB does not delay his throw and is coached to deliver on time.

96

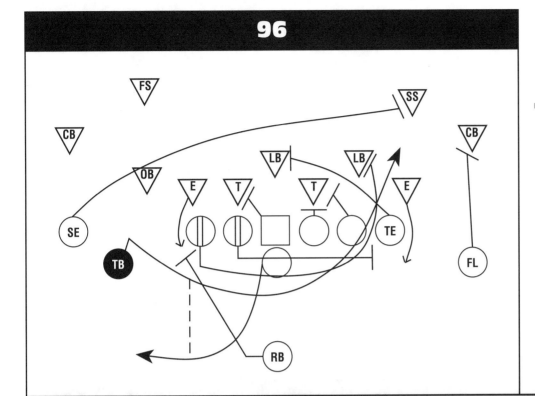

Jimmie Keeling

Hardin-Simmons University

Abilene, Texas

TIAA Conference (NCAA III)

Play Strategy	Player Assignments	Coaching Points

Play Strategy

The play is considered a great first-down call and can be run basically from any spot on the field. The play is most often run into the short side or into the middle of the field. Coach Keeling can set up 96 by running zone stretch and sprint out pass. This is a forward pass play.

Player Assignments

Formation: One-Back

Offensive Linemen

ST: If covered, double combo blocks 4 or 5 technique DT with TE to weakside LB. If uncovered, double combo blocks 1, 2, or 3 technique defender with SG.

SG: If covered, double combo blocks 1, 2, or 3 technique defender with S to weakside LB. If uncovered, down blocks Nose; allows no penetration.

C: If covered, chips and walls off first man backside past the C and on the LOS.

QG: Pulls playside, hugs the LOS, and trap blocks 6, 7, or 9 technique DE (EMOL).

QT: Pulls playside, reads the block of QG; if QG traps DE, QT pulls up 4 or 5 hole. If QG logs DE, pulls outside.

Receivers and Backs

TE: Steps with inside foot, blocks through 4 or 5 technique area to middle or weakside LB. Double combo blocks 4 or 5 technique DT with ST.

SE: Blocks downfield; clears middle third area.

FL: Playside, blocks upfield force. Backside, clears downfield.

RB: Fakes 27, blocks first defender on or outside QT on LOS.

TB: Takes dropstep, releases behind RB, receives forward pass from QB, and follows block of QT.

QB: Fakes 27 with RB, shuttles ball forward to TB, and runs away.

Coaching Points

- The SG blocks Nose from shade weak to shade strong. He must not allow defender to penetrate.

- If the DE squeezes down, the QG log blocks the defender inside, the QT reads the block, runs outside, and turns shoulders upfield to block the first defender to show.

- Key CP to the play. The RB hurries to block the defender, and the ball is passed to the TB directly behind the RB. This hides the ball (forward pass), and the QB continues to roll out away from the playside.

Jim Wacker

University of Minnesota

Minneapolis, Minnesota

Big Ten Conference (1A)

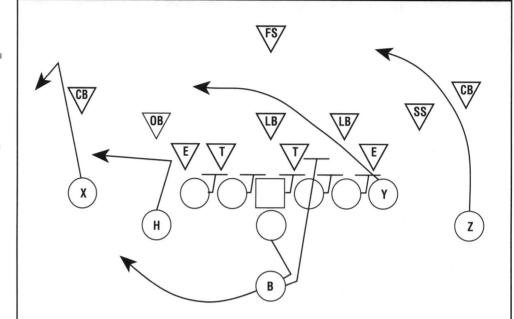

Pro Right 32 Naked

Play Strategy

Coach Wacker likes to use H motion or Z motion because it presents a problem for the defense. This play is called when defensive pursuit is flowing hard to stop the inside running play, and the QB runs the naked boot in a run situation, not in a passing situation. For the play to be successful, the defense must react strongly to the inside fake. It should not be called otherwise.

Player Assignments

Formation: **One-Back**

Offensive Linemen

Offensive linemen have the same blocking assignments as for the run. All five interior linemen run blocks 32. The offensive line positions are called weak or strong depending on the POA.

Receivers and Backs

X: Runs a 22-yard comeback route.

Z: Runs a post route.

H: Sells cutoff block inside; runs flat route at a depth of 3 to 5 yards.

RB: Runs 32 inside zone; makes a great fake with QB.

QB: Runs fake 32 (inside zone) and sells the fake with TB. Boots away from the play (naked). Since the DE is not blocked, the better the fake, the better the execution.

Y: Releases inside, runs inside route across field at a depth of 6 to 8 yards.

Coaching Points

- Both linemen and backs sell inside the zone.

- To set this play up properly, the QB fakes the naked boot when the running play is called inside.

- The H-back steps down as if to block the DE. This tends to slow down his pursuit.

- When facing outside containment, the QB has three receivers within his vision.

Ace Right Jet Strong Z F

64

Joe Petricca

Palatine High School

Palatine, Illinois

Play Strategy	Player Assignments	Coaching Points

Play Strategy

Coach Petricca uses the play early in the game, forcing opponents to defend vertically, while testing deep coverage and personal matchups. If successful, adjustments are used to open up the run and short pass routes. If coverage is unsound or cannot match up, the play may be called in each series throughout the game. The play is also used as an automatic, matched with a specific coverage, matched with another play, or used as a "check-with-me" system at the LOS.

Player Assignments

Formation: **One-Back**

Offensive Linemen

PST: Post blocks end man on LOS, BOB.

PSG: Post blocks next man on LOS, inside FST, BOB.

C: Takes short zone help step playside; hinge blocks.

BSG: Takes short zone help step playside; hinge blocks.

BST: Takes short zone help step playside; hinge blocks.

Receivers and Backs

SE: Runs dig route to the backside seam.

TE: Releases outside; runs seam route.

FL: Releases upfield for 3 steps; works outside on fade.

FB: Off playside hip of C, blocks first threat inside out.

TB: Works to a position between TE and FL, which puts him under the flat defender.

QB: Takes a 3-step drop 5 to 7 yards deep in C/PSG gap.

Coaching Points

■ The PSG and PST, taking a short position step, use the post-block technique. Contact is made on the second step with both fists. This step puts their inside legs (post leg) and shoulders square to the LOS. The punch is designed to neutralize the defender's charge and keep him on the LOS and to the outside. If the defender rushes inside, he is driven down; if the defender rushes outside, they must ride him around the QB.

■ Using the hinge-block technique, the C, BSG, and BST step playside and punch any defender within reach. They must pivot on their playside feet, position their bodies between the QB and defenders, lock on any rusher crossing their faces, and punch the outside numbers while uncoiling and positioning. If no rusher crosses their faces, they sit, look, and help on backside.

■ If deep coverage is cheating playside, the SE is ready for the throwback. The TE looks for the ball on the third step with the width of release depending on who is defending the seam. The FL catches the ball over his inside shoulder while running the fade route.

■ The TB gets to the playside flat, finds an opening, and makes eye contact with the QB ASAP.

■ The QB's presnap key is the flat defender. On his third step, the QB throws on time inside to the TE or outside to the FL.

Dave Roberts

Northeastern Louisiana

Monroe, Louisiana

(1989–1993)

Southland Conference
(1AA)

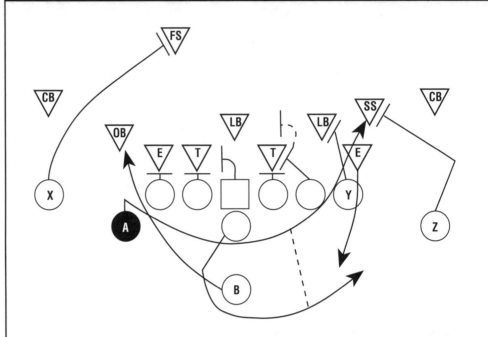

Left 5 Naked Pitch

Play Strategy	Player Assignments	Coaching Points

Play Strategy

Coach Roberts likes to use this shuffle pass on third down plays needing 5 yards or more, against teams that show certain pass coverages for second and long situations, and against teams that rush the strongside DE to contain the QB. Coach Roberts believes that the QB fake to the weak side and the reversal of field are deceiving to the DE.

Player Assignments

Formation: **One-Back**

Offensive Linemen

ST: Secures the area, pushes DT, and releases to near LB.

SG: Base blocks DT.

C: Secures middle, checks for middle LB, and turns back to help QG.

QG: Base blocks DT.

QT: Base blocks DE.

Receivers and Backs

X: Releases to cut off FS.

Z: Releases and blocks SS.

Y: Allows DE to come upfield to contain QB. Releases inside to block strongside LB.

B: Fakes weakside dive (5). Secures area for weakside LB.

A: Hesitates 1 count, which allows B to fake dive. Runs behind the offensive line and looks for soft pitch from QB.

QB: Fronts out to B and makes a good fake. Reverses field and gets depth, as he expects DE to contain. Pitches the ball to A as he runs under DE's containment technique.

Coaching Points

■ This shuffle play has A running naked. There are no lead blockers.

■ After faking to the weak side, the QB turns to the strong side, where he must gain depth to influence the DE upfield. This creates a running lane for A. Then, after reading the DE, the QB pitches forward to A.

■ Key blocks are made by the TE, who blocks and seals off the strong LB, and Z, who blocks off the SS.

Slot Shovel Right

Lou Tepper

University of Illinois

Champaign, Illinois

Big Ten Conference (1A)

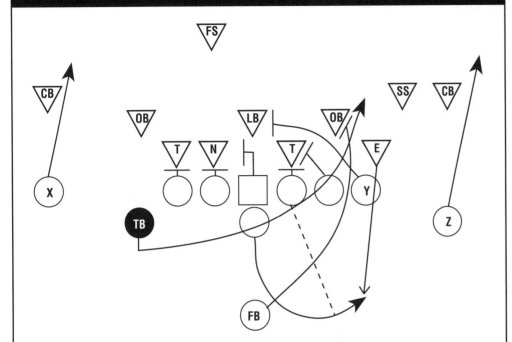

Play Strategy	Player Assignments	Coaching Points

Play Strategy

This play is most effective when the defense is expecting a pass and is applying pressure from the outside. A plus arises from the turnback protection provided by the line, which uses the same technique employed in sprint out passing. This play also helps to control the scrape LBs, who are coming on fast. Strategy plays an important role in the use of the shovel pass because it provides another way to get the ball to the corner.

Player Assignments

Formation: **One-Back**

Offensive Linemen

It is an advantage of the offensive linemen that all have the same basic blocking assignment, the turnback block. With all linemen blocking in the same direction, the DL has only one way to rush the QB. Versus 40 is an exception, as the PSG/PST double teams DT. The playside DE is not blocked.

Receivers and Backs

X: Sells the 8 route. Blocks deep 1/2 or deep 1/3.

Y: Blocks middle to backside LB.

Z: Sells the 8 route. Blocks deep 1/2 or deep 1/3.

FB: Sells the sprint out action. Blocks first LB from C/PSG gap out.

TB: Slotted, runs playside, receives shovel pass from QB, sprints upfield.

QB: Sells the sprint out action, tries to break containment, and shovels ball under to TB.

Coaching Points

■ The wide receivers, FB, TB, and QB are taught to sell the spring-out attack, which resembles an outside play.

■ The QB open steps in the direction of the sprint out and convinces the defenders responsible for containment that it's going to be a pass.

■ The timing between the TB and the QB shovel pass depends on how much pressure is put on to contain the QB. The TB must be ready to receive the pitch quickly.

Terry Allen

Northern Iowa University

Cedar Falls, Iowa

Gateway Conference (1AA)

528

Play Strategy

The play can be called on any down and distance. However, if the defense is playing cover 3, this play (549) will be called to the left side. At times, depending on the defensive front, either or both guards may pull, which makes it look like a running play.

Player Assignments

Formation: **Split Backs**

Offensive Linemen

OST: Blocks first lineman on or outside.

OSG: Blocks first lineman inside, on, or pulls to block outside of OST.

C: Blocks lineman on or away, leads to onside gap, slides out, and double checks inside LB to outside LB.

BSG: Blocks lineman on or outside, pulls 3 steps onside; pivots to check inside LB to outside LB.

BST: Hinge blocks first lineman on or outside.

Receivers and Backs

X: Versus hard corner fade, runs a post go route. If X is called, he becomes primary receiver.

Z: Versus hard corner fade, runs an 18-yard out route.

Y: Releases outside; runs seam route.

FB: Fakes sweep; checks for onside LB blitz to EMOL.

HB: Runs load course for 2 steps; quickly breaks off to flat.

QB: Opens playside to the hole, gains depth with first step, and reads strong OB.

Coaching Points

■ Versus 50 defensive front, OST and OSG tag block. BST will make "blue" or "red" call if two defenders are outside and on the LOS.

■ Versus 70 defensive front (double eagle), line makes "gold" or "purple" calls.

■ If 528X is called, X becomes the primary receiver on a post go route.

■ QB is coached not to ball fake or look at the back. The FB runs by and fakes.

■ FB cheats over and back for correct alignment.

49 Rail

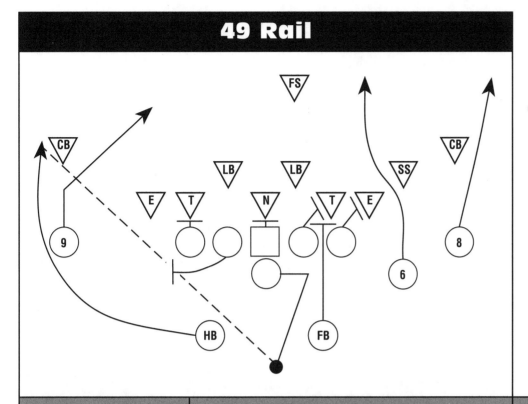

Joe Miller

New Hanover High School

Wilmington, North Carolina

Play Strategy	Player Assignments	Coaching Points

Play Strategy

This play can be run at any time from the hash-mark. The back, who comes out of the back-field and runs the side-line route, puts pressure on defensive coverage. This is especially true for the dropoff ends or LBs who are assigned back out of the backfield. The inside fake keeps the inside LBs from reading pass.

Player Assignments

Formation: **Split Backs**

Offensive Linemen

ST: With "fan" call, blocks first man outside.

SG: With "fan" call, blocks first man outside.

C: Blocks Nose; if uncovered, helps WG.

WG: If covered, blocks big on big ("boy" call). If uncovered, checks for LB and steps out to block DE.

WT: Blocks big on big.

Receivers and Backs

#9: (SE) Releases upfield; runs a strong post route.

#8: (SE) Runs a deep fly route.

#6: (SB) Releases inside; runs a seam route up the middle.

FB: Runs veer action through B gap; blocks near LB.

HB: Releases outside, runs rail route, and becomes primary receiver.

QB: Steps strong side, fakes inside veer to FB, drops back 3 steps, sets feet, and throws to HB.

Coaching Points

- If the LB threatens, the WG stays and blocks him so that the QB is able to execute a fake and drop back.

- To keep the sideline area open, the boundary CB needs to bite on the post route run by #9.

- Both #6 and #8 need to convince coverage that the ball is going to be thrown their way.

- After the FB fake, the QB drops back 3 steps, turns, and throws to HB.

Frosty Westering

Pacific Lutheran University

Parkland, Washington

Columbia Conference
(NAIA)

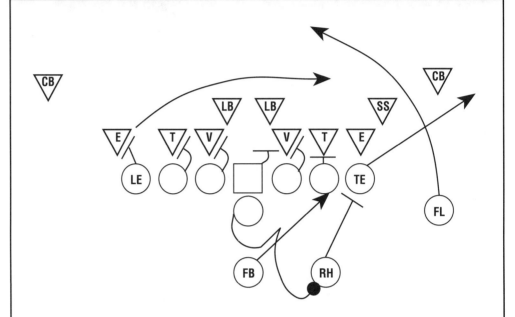

Flackin Right

Play Strategy

Although it may be run anywhere on the field, the play action is most effective inside the opponent's 10-yard line. It is an advantage that this play can be used in various formations, such as the slot or full house.

Player Assignments

Formation: **Split Backs Strong**

Offensive Linemen

RT: Blocks man over, outside.

RG: Steps playside gap; blocks first defender to show.

C: Steps playside gap; blocks first defender to show.

LG: Steps playside gap; blocks first defender to show.

LT: Steps playside gap; blocks first defender to show.

Receivers and Backs

LE: Blocks man over inside or outside for 1 count; runs drag route across middle.

TE: Slow blocks man over or outside defender for 2 counts. Slants out to corner of the end zone.

FL: Releases inside at 45-degree angle with outside hand up; runs for near side of the goal post. Approximately 5 yards from goal post, stops and pivots, slides to the outside.

FB: Runs off-tackle slant at modified speed, ball fakes, and blocks out on defender in his path.

RH: Blocks first man to show over, inside, or outside TE.

QB: Reverse pivots or steps out to FB, fakes belly ride for 2 seconds, pulls ball, sets feet, reads defense, and throws to open receiver for touchdown.

Coaching Points

■ Key to the play's success is an excellent maneuver by the FL while running the two dimensional pass route.

■ The FB leans forward as the ball is put in the belly ride position. The FB's timing with the QB needs to sell the run.

■ The action of the TE during the slow block and release is hard for a defense to read. If he is covered tightly, the TE breaks quickly to the end zone line.

■ Regular blocking rules for zone or man fit all defenses that are not playing goal line.

■ This is a play action pass, not a pick. All the routes run can be open.

80 X-Out

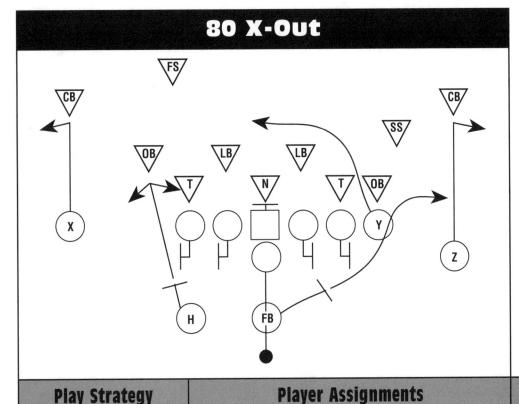

Bill Mallory

Indiana University

Bloomington, Indiana

Big Ten Conference (1A)

Play Strategy	Player Assignments	Coaching Points

Play Strategy

The dropback pass play is called in any given situation. This high-percentage pass is effective against any coverage. Coach Mallory likes to throw from the hashmark or in the middle. The TB's check release gives the QB another passing option. The 80 X-Out is just one of many routes that can be run from the 80 series.

Player Assignments

Formation: **Pro**

Offensive Linemen

FST: If covered, set blocks; if uncovered, set blocks outside.

FSG: If covered, set blocks; if uncovered, combo blocks with C.

C: Combo blocks frontside. Versus even, combo blocks with both guards.

BSG: Fan blocks. (Blocking man protection, count defenders inside out, first down lineman from C out.)

BST: Fan blocks on second down lineman, counting inside out from C.

Receivers and Backs

X: Releases outside, runs curl route at depth of 12 to 14 yards, and runs 10 to 12 yards against blitz.

Y: Releases outside, runs dig route at depth of 10 to 12 yards, and runs 10 yards against blitz.

Z: Releases outside, runs curl route at depth of 12 to 14 yards, and runs 10 to 12 yards against blitz.

H: Checks outside pressure weakside; runs short option route at 4 yards.

F: Checks outside pressure strong side; runs short option route at 4 yards.

QB: Takes a 5-step drop, executes progression read, and throws to X, H, or Y.

Coaching Points

■ FST sets up to block defender head up, inside, or outside shoulder.

■ If uncovered, the FSG steps for hip of Nose, keeps shoulders square, closes the gap, and keys the Nose's reactions. If Nose plays straight or angles to the play, the FSG keeps him on LOS; if Nose angles away, he keys the LB.

■ X, running the out route, is the primary receiver. If he is not open, the QB looks to the H-back option route, and finally looks to Y running the dig route across the field.

■ Fan blocking is man protection except on radical moves by the defense. In that case, special blocking rules apply.

Spike Dykes

Texas Tech University

Lubbock, Texas

Southwest Conference
(1A)

71 B Option

Play Strategy

Running a balanced attack, Coach Dykes likes the 71 B Option as a good short-yardage play that can be used any time. In his offset I-formation, the FB running upfield as a pass receiver acts to slow down the defensive rush on that side. If the defense shows cover 2, the QB knows that X will run the fade route and can throw to him immediately. On any down, the use of five receivers puts an added strain on all defensive coverages.

Player Assignments

Formation: **Off-Set I-Formation**

Offensive Linemen

RT: If covered, blocks man on; if uncovered, blocks first man on LOS, outside.

RG: If covered, blocks man on; if uncovered, sets and checks for near LB.

C: If covered, blocks Nose; if uncovered, sets and checks for near LB.

LG: If covered, blocks man on; if uncovered, sets and checks for near LB.

LT: If covered, blocks man on; if uncovered, blocks first man on LOS, outside.

Receivers and Backs

X: Runs a 3-count out route. Versus cover 2, runs a fade route.

Y: Releases outside; runs a 4-count corner route.

Z: Pushes hard upfield to depth of 6 yards; executes a sharp break inside or out according to coverage.

TB: Check backside for OB; runs flare route.

FB: Pushes hard upfield to depth of 6 yards; breaks off inside or outside.

QB: Presnap reads the FS through the weakside LB.

Coaching Points

■ In the short passing game, the line blocks against any defensive front.

■ The FB is designated as the "hot" receiver. He is on the same side as the weakside LB.

■ To run the correct route, each receiver reads either under or deep coverage.

■ The QB takes a 3-step drop while reading the FS. He is ready to throw the hot if the weakside LB blitzes.

49 Tailback Screen

Dick Dullaghan

Ben Davis High School

Indianapolis, Indiana

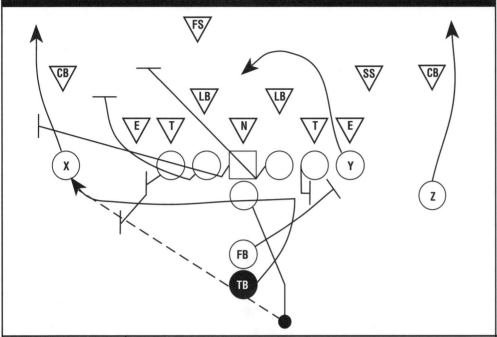

Play Strategy

There is no hesitation on Coach Dullaghan's part to call this TB screen pass in any long-yardage situation. A good time to call this play is when facing a weakside heavy pass rush, especially by the DE. With the two wideouts running streak routes and the Y hooking inside, the defense thinks downfield pass.

Player Assignments

Formation: **I-Formation**

Offensive Linemen

ST: Blocks 40 protection.

SG: Begins blocking 40 protection, waits for C's go call, and sprints weakside flat, angling at a depth of 6 to 8 yards.

C: Blocks 40 protection, counts 1001, 1002, 1003, then yells go. Sprints flat across QG's face and straight down the line. After passing QG, gets 7 yards deep to block run support defender in flat.

QG: Blocks 40 protection, waits for C to cross face, and sprints to the weakside flat angling at a depth of 4 to 6 yards. Looks to block FS or frontside LB.

QT: Blocks 40 protection, locks on, and rides the DE to a depth of 7 yards. At 7 yards, executes crossbody block with his head to the outside.

Receivers and Backs

X: Takes a maximum split; runs a streak route.

Y: Hooks over middle at 10 yards; looks for ball.

Z: Takes a maximum split; runs a streak route.

FB: Blocks 40 protection.

TB: Blocks 40 protection, attacks strongside B gap, butts up frontside LB if he blitzes, and slips into weak flat 2 yards behind the LOS and 5 yards outside the QT. Looks inside, catches ball; runs off of C's block on run support.

QB: Makes 40 pass set. Looks deep, retreats 3 to 4 more yards, and throws to TB in weakside flat.

Coaching Points

- When the CBs break down, X and Z stalk block. X and Z streak to sell the CB on a deep pass.

- If the ball is not thrown to Y, he runs a cutoff block on the backside LB at the second level.

- In the weakside flat, SG, C, and QG are coached to block the first wrong colored jersey that shows.

- It is important for the QT to get the DE off his feet. The OT accomplishes the block by crashing his torso hard into the DE's feet. Merely "falling" on the DE's feet is not enough.

73

Dennis Erickson

University of Miami

Coral Gables, Florida

Big East Conference
(1A)

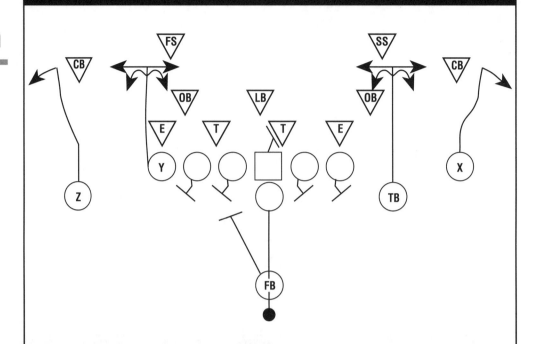

Doubles Left 71X

Play Strategy

This pass is used with 70 protection. Doubles 71X can be run against any coverage and is often used as a first-down play. Another situation where it is used is for third down, 8 to 10 yards. The field position preference is in the middle of the field. If they are on the hash, both the TB and X are put on the wide side. The use of motion across to the opposite side of alignment has been effective: Z from trips, TB from trey, and Y from trey off.

Player Assignments

Formation: **One-Back**

Offensive Linemen (70 protection)

ST: Keys man over. If uncovered, fans to Sam LB.

SG: Keys man over. If uncovered, turns to Nose.

C: Keys Nose. If uncovered, turns to Mike LB.

WG: Keys man over. If uncovered, turns to #2 weak side.

WT: Keys man over. If #3 weak side moves on LOS, alerts out call.

Receivers and Backs

X: Runs a 14-yard out.

Y: Runs 8 to 10 yard option; reads hot. If ST is covered and Sam and Buck blitz, reads hot. If ST is covered and Mike and Buck blitz, reads hot.

Z: Runs a 14-yard out.

FB: If ST is covered, keys Buck to Sam to block. If ST is uncovered, keys Buck to Mike to block.

TB: Runs 8 to 10 yard option.

QB: Keeps presnap coverage. (a) X on out, (b) TB on option (c) Z on out, (d) Y on option.

Coaching Points

■ In cover 2, it is important for X/Z to convert outs to takeoffs. They must release the outside defender.

■ The QB's presnap reads are stressed daily.

■ The QB and option route receivers must be aware of robber coverage. They are coached to avoid the robber and must sit down in route instead.

■ Versus nickle and double eagle defenses, FB blocking rules vary according to the game plan.

Doubles Right 168 Shallow/Wide

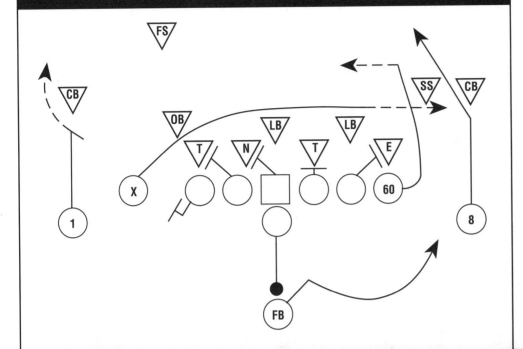

Jim Donnan

Marshall University

Huntington, West Virginia

Southern Conference (1AA)

Play Strategy

This play is called when long yardage (+20) is needed, not during a particular down. The on-field reads by the four receivers are effective against man or zone. Coach Donnan believes that this play is tough to stop, especially if the QB and his receivers are on the same page.

Player Assignments

Formation: **One-Back**

Offensive Linemen

LT: Slides left, blocks outside, and looks for DE.

LG: Slide left; blocks outside.

C: Blocks man on or slides left; blocks outside.

RG: Blocks man on.

RT: Blocks outside; looks for DE.

Receivers and Backs

FL(1): Aligns on top of field numbers. Runs 8-yard hitch route; against tight corner, runs fade.

SE: Splits distance between LT and FL; runs shallow route across field.

TE: #60 in play description. Releases outside and upfield, reads coverage settle down or run across vs. man.

FL(8): Aligns on top of field numbers; runs a deep post route.

FB: Checks playside for LB blitz. If not, runs wide route.

QB: Drops back; reads LBs and safeties for man or zone.

Coaching Points

■ It is important that all four receivers release free and get into their reads.

■ If both LBs blitz, the FB takes the most dangerous one, and the QB hits the shallow route quickly.

■ If both LBs drop into coverage, the FB runs his wide route.

■ TE sight adjusts #5 strong; backside FL sight adjusts #4 weak to determine zone or man coverage.

■ Versus man or blitz, the QB throws the post route. He can also throw to the FB.

75

Tom Grippa

Elder High School
Cincinnati, Ohio

82 Up

Play Strategy	Player Assignments	Coaching Points

Play Strategy

This is a good first- or second-down call because, although it has big-play potential, it is a high-percentage play. Coach Grippa likes this weakside passing series because it has proven successful against high school coverages that defend flat and hook zones.

Player Assignments

Formation: **One-Back**

Offensive Linemen

PST: If covered, blocks BOB. If uncovered, blocks out to next defender on LOS.

PSG: If covered, blocks BOB. If covered by LB, blocks LB to double on Nose.

C: Blocks O to playside LB.

BSG: If covered, blocks BOB. If uncovered, blocks out on next defender on LOS.

BST: Blocks #3.

Receivers and Backs

X: Runs 10 to 12 yard curl route; vs. zone finds the hole between flat defender and hook zone. If WLB widens his drop, goes to second hole in between LBs.

Z: Runs a backside route, keeps FS in 3-deep coverage from robbing the curl, and vs. 2 deep runs through the middle of the field.

Y: Blocks EMOL, runs an outside choice 5 yards deep, 1 yard outside ends alignment. Runs a flat route vs. man.

A: Versus some opponents blocks #4. If #4 drops, runs an up route; once outside of X, runs vertical course on the numbers.

B: If BSG is covered, blocks OB. If BSG is uncovered (LB over BSG), blocks inside LB. If LB drops, runs circle route.

QB: Takes a 5-step drop, passing progression is A - X - B. On the third step, looks at A. If open, throws the up route. If A is covered, immediately looks to throw to X on curl route. If X is covered, throws to B on the circle route.

Coaching Points

- The 80 series uses man protection. It can be blocked against 50, eagle weak, 43, 44, or other fronts.

- Against man, X separates from his defender and runs horizontally across the field. A is taught to run the up route in a banana-like course, gaining width and depth.

- In trips, Z's route can serve as a pick on the WLB. Z keeps deep coverage from getting on the curl.

- The QB is trained to look through the goal post at the snap and for his first 3 steps.

- When the defense rushes 4 weak side, B blocks the WLB to OB. A must stay to block the OB. If the WLB or OLB rushes, A releases to run the up route.

- When the WLB has to cover A, the coach prefers to play against man coverage. If the 83 Up is called, the TE is on the left.

40 Y/A Option

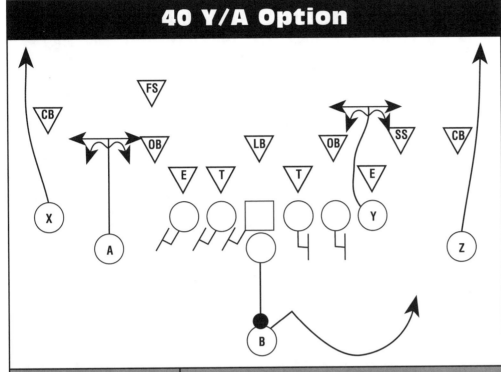

Jerry Schliem

Milton High School

Milton, Wisconsin

Play Strategy	Player Assignments	Coaching Points

Play Strategy

The hot series of Coach Schliem's passing attack is based on vertical and horizontal stretch. This play can be used at any time, especially against pressing defenses. The 40 Y/A Option can be run from a variety of formations.

Player Assignments

Formation: **One-Back**

Offensive Linemen

The 40/50 protection package is a four-man pattern that allows a back to free release weak side.

RT: Solid call, blocks man on. Fan call, blocks outside.

RG: Solid call, blocks man on. Fan call, blocks inside. If uncovered, blocks inside.

C: Fan call, blocks weak side. Otto call, checks weakside gap. Slide call, blocks man on LG.

RG: Otto call, blocks outside. Fan call, blocks outside. Slide call, blocks man on.

RT: Otto call, blocks outside. Fan call, blocks outside. Slide call, blocks DE.

Receivers and Backs

X: Releases outside; runs streak route.

Y: Runs option route to depth of 10 yards.

Z: Release outside; runs streak route.

A: Releases outside; runs option route to depth of 6 yards.

B: Looks to block strong inside LB to strongside OB. If not, runs swing route.

QB: Takes 5-step drop big or 3-step drop quick.

Coaching Points

■ Y works to release free. As hot receiver, he looks for ball if the LBs blitz. Y and A read option area for zone or man coverage. If zone, turns away from nearest defender; if man, runs away.

■ While running the streak route, X and Y run an adjustment fade route within 3 yards of the boundary.

■ B is the QB's third check. B must take his time before releasing weak side.

■ The QB's progression reads are A, Y, and B. Versus zone, he throws quickly to the shoulder away from the nearest defender. Versus man, he allows receiver to run away. Versus 2 deep, he checks X's fade route to A's option route.

77

Jack Stark

Shelton High School

Shelton, Washington

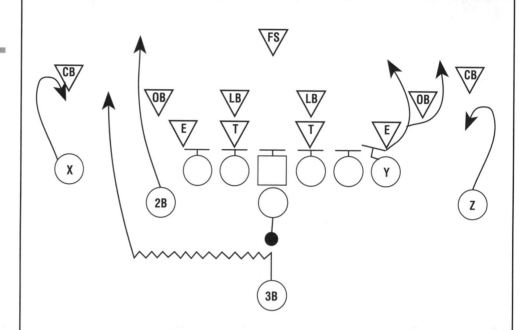

Dubs Right 93X-Divide

Play Strategy

This play can be used in both short- and long-yardage situations. When it is necessary to move the chains or there is a need to take care of LB blitzes, the 93 X-divide is called. By incorporating the short passing game within the spread offense, most defenses are balanced. The 3B in motion creates a no-back look for the defense. The defense must adjust, or the QB can go to the open receiver. The two CBs are forced into man because of the hitch route in front.

Player Assignments

Formation: **One-Back**

Offensive Linemen

The #1 priority for the line is to protect the QB. To produce consistency and reduce confusion, the 90 protection package is used. All linemen are to block man on or up and then block the inside gap. The C blocks either gap, depending on the most dangerous defender.

Receivers and Backs

Y: Checks inside gap; releases outside and upfield, depending on the OB alignment.

X: Releases outside; runs a 6-yard hitch route.

Z: Releases outside; runs a 6-yard hitch route.

2B: Releases outside; runs an up route.

3B: Runs in motion to XE; turns upfield on snap.

QB: Takes 3-step drop; checks to see which defender moves with motion.

Coaching Points

■ Both wide receivers are spread horizontally to create more passing lanes.

■ Before running the hitch, the X and Z are coached to sell the fade route.

■ The 2B becomes a hot receiver if the LB blitzes. He must look inside for the quick pass.

■ While in motion, the 3B turns upfield when he sees X release off the LOS, not the QB's cadence. When upfield, the 3B must look for a quick pass from the QB.

■ The ball is snapped when the 3B is 2 steps outside the 2B. This creates a split between X and the 2B.

Spread Right Rip 60 Go

78

Alan Paturzo

Wagner High School
Staten Island, New York

Play Strategy	Player Assignments	Coaching Points

Play Strategy

The play is best run from the hashmark. The wide side gives the receiver running room after the catch. The use of motion forces defensive coverages to show. Since Coach Paturzo likes to throw quickly off a SS read vs. zone, it works best vs. 2 deep. However, it can be run against any coverage. Variations include going backside, running a super screen, or deep-crossing routes.

Player Assignments

Formation: **One-Back**

Offensive Linemen

The 60 pass protection package involves five linemen and the SB, when needed. The blocking rules are the same for blocking the odd or even front. Base rule: playside blocks man on, over, inside. Backside blocks inside, on, over. If no defender comes, all linemen help block backside. Versus 70 front, 80 protection is used.

Receivers and Backs

SE: Versus 3 deep, runs streak route, gets the CB to turn and run. Versus 2 deep, releases outside, runs fade/corner route, involves the half safety.

TE: Versus 3 deep or 2 deep, runs flat route, looks for ball on third step. If not, gets width and extends the route. Versus blitz, #1 receiver looks over inside shoulder immediately for ball.

FL: Versus 3 deep, wide split, runs streak route, clears zone for TE extension. Versus 2 deep, runs fade route, occupies CB and SS.

TB: Goes in motion, vs. 3 deep turns up 5 yards outside TE, looks for ball in seam if SS gets wide. If not, extends route, reacts to FS. Versus 2 deep, turns and reads the SS.

QB: Versus 3 deep, on third step reads SS. If SS widens, throws to TB, not open drops to 5 step. Now, looks inside to TB to outside TE. Versus 2 deep, on third step looks for TE. If not open, drops to 5 step; looks for TE over middle. Versus 2-deep man, looks to TB cutting across middle, then back to TE.

SB: Checks for MLB or first defender off the corner. Versus odd, cut blocks #3. Versus even, helps playside RT to outside.

Coaching Points

- QB must be able to preread coverages.

- If ball is not thrown on third step, all receivers run route extensions.

- The TB's motion adjusts to coverage and helps put defenders on an island; sets up picks on release.

- If necessary, the TB can use a back-and-forth motion behind the LOS.

- The play softens the curl defender with a vertical outside release and softens the hard corner by forcing the outside release. Then, with running room, the ball is thrown to TE.

79

Steve Axman

Northern Arizona University

Flagstaff, Arizona

Big Sky Conference (1AA)

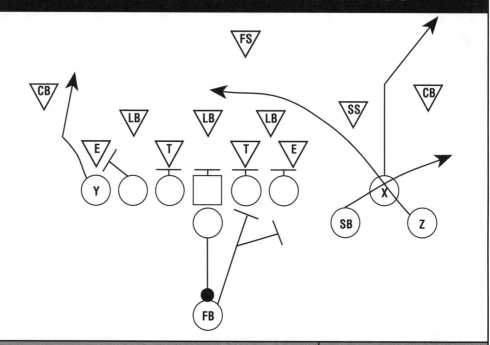

Left Cat Bunch 247 Pivot

Play Strategy	Player Assignments	Coaching Points

Play Strategy

The bunch series is run on any down as a short-yardage play. It also may be used to throw deep. The sight adjustment receivers in this play give the QB an option to handle blitzes from both sides. All three eligible receivers line up close to each other. All release and run crossing routes, putting extra pressure on defensive coverages. Another way to run the play is from the wing formation, where the FB comes out into the flat.

Player Assignments

Formation: **One-Back**

Offensive Linemen

BST: Blocks BOB.

BSG: Blocks BOB.

C: If covered, blocks BOB. If uncovered, checks backside LB and blocks backside gap.

BSG: If covered, blocks BOB. If uncovered, checks backside LB and blocks inside gap.

BST: If covered, blocks BOB. If uncovered, blocks backside DE.

Receivers and Backs

X: Runs hook route (12 yards) or corner route straight upfield.

Y: Runs a backside hitch route at depth of 5 yards.

Z: Runs pivot route, runs hard down inside, and slides into a hole at depth of 5 yards.

SB: Runs arrow route to flat.

FB: Double reads; blocks first inside LB to second outside LB playside.

QB: Takes a 5-step drop; follows QB progression keys.

Coaching Points

- Y becomes the hot or sight receiver to the backside.

- The SB becomes the hot or sight receiver to the bunch side.

- In running the pivot route, Z must let X go first to avoid making contact.

- It is important for X to get a clean release upfield. He breaks off at 12 yards and runs the corner route, which is the primary route.

- First, the QB is aware of beating the backside blitz with Y as hot receiver in the flat. QB progression reads are as follows: (a) Looks to throw to X running the corner route. (b) Z, in the middle, slides to get open in the hole between the LBs.

Red Right 86 X Post

80

John Mackovic

University of Texas

Austin, Texas

Southwest Conference
(1A)

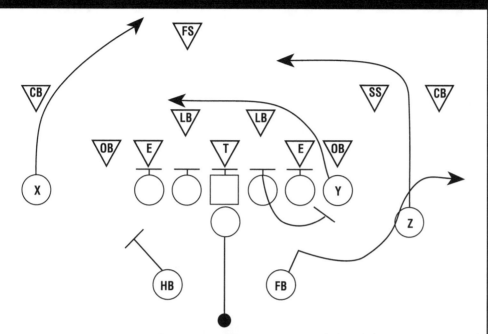

Play Strategy	Player Assignments	Coaching Points

Play Strategy

Use this all-purpose pass play on first and third downs. It can be used deep inside your own territory or inside the red zone. The play is primarily designed to hit Z on the deep square-in pattern between the LBs and the secondary. While it is possible to use various motions, it has been a better play when everyone is set before the snap of the ball. When different formations are used, receivers' routes are influenced by their alignment in the formation rather than by the position they play. Whenever the safety vacates the middle of the field, the QB looks for the XE going through the post for the TD.

Player Assignments

Formation: **Split Backs**

Offensive Linemen

ST: Blocks man over.

SG: Double reads LB if he blitzes. If not, goes to the end of the line and blocks EMOL.

C: Blocks man over.

WG: Blocks LB if he blitzes. If not, helps C in the middle.

WT: Blocks man over.

Receivers and Backs

X: Runs deep post route through the safety area, breaks at 10 to 12 yards. Clears through the safety area with speed.

Y: Runs crossing route through the linebacker area, breaks at 10 yards and, if possible, gets behind the LBs. If forced to go under the LBs, gets to the 10-yard level.

Z: Runs deep square, breaks at 14-16 yards, never deeper than 18-20 yards. Expects ball in any area if open.

HB: Blocks weakside EMOL.

FB: Double reads LB with SG. If LB blitzes and SG takes him, goes to the end of the line. If LB does not blitz, he is free to release into the flat route, fans at 5 to 7 yards, and does not pass field numbers.

QB: Presnap reads for any possible blitz. At snap, he checks safety area for post route by XE. Reads LB drop vs. the deep square-in. If LBs have been pulled with the TE and FB, delivers to Z receiver. If LBs have continued to drop with depth to cover the deep square-in, he lays off to the FB.

Coaching Points

■ Versus blitz, the QB sets up on five steps (7 yards); vs. zone, seven steps (10 yards). Special attention is given by the QB to reading the coverages. He throws accordingly.

■ Depending on down and distance, the QB reads the pass from deep to short.

■ All receivers must be in proper alignment with each other to create a pull on the defense.

■ LB drops determine whether the QB throws to Z or to the crossing route of Y.

■ The FB helps pull the LBs wide by his route. If the LBs do not react and allow Z to get open, the QB throws to the FB.

■ An alternate flare route run by the FB is good against teams who focus on stopping the flare pass or stopping screens to the backs.

81

LaVell Edwards

Brigham Young

Provo, Utah

Western Athletic
Conference (1A)

Split Right 958

| Play Strategy | Player Assignments | Coaching Points |

Play Strategy

This all-purpose pass play is a good first-down call. This is especially true if you're unsure of the defensive coverage. This play can be used regardless of the defense, because it provides a strongside vertical stretch. Also, with the use of maximum protection and different routes, this play tests all coverages. Coach Edwards believes in throwing the ball upfield, but he likes to keep safety valve receivers in short-yardage routes. If defense insists on keeping SS to the wide side, the formation will be put into the sideline.

Player Assignments

Formation: **Split Backs**

Offensive Linemen

Pass protection is set up so that the offensive line, from tackle to tackle, has the responsibility of blocking inside. Knowing that the backs have the responsibility of picking up all defenders outside the tackles, all five linemen block base.

Receivers and Backs

X: Splits and heads for FS.

Y: Sail route vs. zone; drag route vs. man.

Z: Runs streak route to beat CB.

RH: Checks; runs arrow route.

LH: Checks; runs rip route.

QB: Takes a 5-step drop with hitch step. By progression: (a) QB looks for Z to see whether he has beaten CB; (b) looks to SS to read throwing keys (if he stays high for Y, he throws to RH; if he breaks to the flat, he goes to Y); (c) if FS attempts to get to Y, he throws to X behind.

Coaching Points

■ As the primary receiver, Y takes easy release and reads coverage. If against a zone, he stays high in an imaginary spot where the zones meet. If against man, he runs at SS, fakes inside, and goes hard outside 12 to 15 yards. If he is not open, the QB will come off to someone else.

■ The QB is coached to avoid forcing the ball into coverage. Emphasis is placed on following progression keys.

■ Halfbacks must be prepared to block low and hard at the outside rush before releasing into their assigned routes.

74-75 Double Seam

Tom Coughlin

Jacksonville

(NFL)

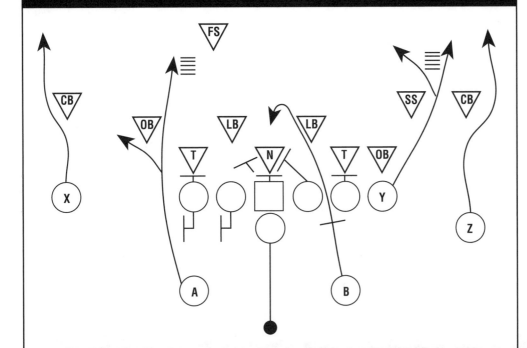

Play Strategy	Player Assignments	Coaching Points

Play Strategy

This play is effective on any given down because of built-in flare control. In the single back concept, the hots and sights are built in to take off pressure and find misalignments. The QB is always looking for a mismatch when he reads man coverage. While using 70 protection, the strategy of using different formations creates problems for the defense.

Player Assignments

Formation: **Split Backs**

Offensive Linemen (Slide Protection)

FST: Base #1 on; fans to #2.

FSG: Slides if uncovered. Base #1 on LOS (no slide).

C: Slides for backside A gap to Jack LB. If uncovered, goes backside for next LB.

BSG: If uncovered, blocks Will LB, base #1 on. Possibly fans BST if Will LB is on LOS.

BST: Base #1; fans to #2.

Receivers and Backs

X: Executes a go route, expands the field, 6 yards from the sideline.

Z: Depending on alignment, executes a go or seam route.

Y: Executes seam read vs. 3-deep or man coverage, vs. 2-deep will split the two safeties.

A: Weakside back has free release.

B: Remaining back checks Mike to Sam. If they don't come, releases to designated route.

QB: Drops back with presnap reads, throws off progression.

Coaching Points

■ A basic premise in vertical stretch is to put four receivers upfield as fast as possible and divide the deep coverage.

■ The two outside receivers are coached against 3-deep coverage to release on go routes. Against 2 deep, they run fade routes and against man, they run to win on go route.

■ The most common defense fronts seen are 3-4 and 4-3.

■ Y's seam route is 2 yards outside the hashmark; hot receiver if Mike LB or Sam LB come strong.

83

Jim Caldwell

Wake Forest University

Winston-Salem, North Carolina

Atlantic Coast Conference (1A)

52 Stop

Play Strategy

Coach Caldwell's 52 Stop comes from the 50s package. Use this play when a medium pass play is needed. To learn how the linebackers are assigned, this is especially good as a 1st and 10 selection. The vertical stretch pressures the defense to react to the pass. If in man coverage, this provides an excellent runaway opportunity for Y to cross the field with B in the flat. If in zone, Y and B should settle down in open space, facing the QB. The opponent's inside LBs will be put to the test with the 52 Stop.

Player Assignments

Formation: **Split Backs**

Offensive Linemen

ST: Blocks Okie and stack tackle (big).

SG: Blocks Okie LB to Nose. Zone stacks with C. Blocks (big) for all other defenses.

C: Over, longside; blocks shortside vs. state defense (4 short).

LG: Blocks Okie LB to Sam (double read). Blocks (big) if not Okie. If free, helps C.

LT: Blocks Okie tackle. Blocks (big) if not Okie.

Receivers and Backs

X: Minimum split is 10 yards. Runs a seam post route (12-yard break).

Y: If possible, runs an inside release, runs a 5 to 7 yard hook, in SG/C gap, and continues across the field vs. man.

Z: Minimum split. Runs an in-lane route (16-yards deep).

A: Blocks 50 protection.

B: Runs a spot route (5 yards wide x 5 yards deep).

QB: Executes a 5-step drop.

Coaching Points

- Both wideouts (X and Z) are coached to take a minimum split of 10 yards. Upon release, they must distinguish between zone and man coverages.

- Z must throttle down in the open area on the in-lane route. He is the secondary receiver in good view of the QB.

- B releases to a spot 5 yards wide and 5 yards deep. He must face the QB. In man with the LB, he breaks to the flat. He is the third choice of the QB.

- It is very critical for Y to release inside as the primary receiver.

- The QB, on the 5-step drop, uses a Y, Z, B pass progression read. If Y is open, he uses a hit (on the 5th step) and throws. If Y is covered, he takes a small hitch and throws to Z or B.

- This dropback protection has the backs reading linebacker checks.

Brown 538 Angle

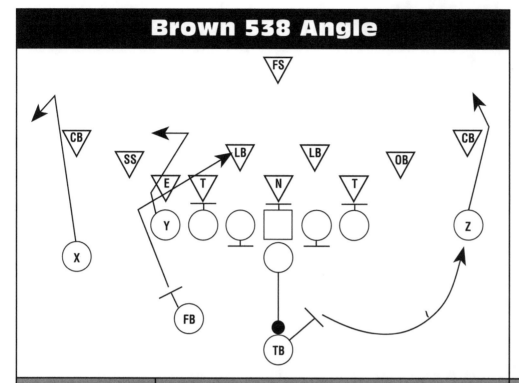

Bruce Snyder

Arizona State University

Tempe, Arizona

Pac-10 Conference (1A)

Play Strategy

Coach Snyder calls the 538 Angle vs. a 3-deep or 2-deep zone. The play is a home run throw to Z on any given down. If it's not there, the QB progression reads from the TE to the RB to pick up the necessary yardage. If the defense plays man, the Z's post route and the TE's crossing route are there for the pickings. The FB also can beat the LBs on the angle route.

Player Assignments

Formation: **Split Backs**

Offensive Linemen

RT: Stick blocks; is alert for possible KC call.

RG: Blocks zone; is ready for possible gap call; is alert for KC, Rose/Lou, or over Rose/Lou calls.

C: Blocks zone; is ready for possible over call. If both A gaps are threatened, possible Rose/Lou call. Man sets when uncovered unless QB signals trump Rose/Lou calls.

LG: Blocks zone, is ready for possible gap call. Is alert for KC, Rose/Lou, or over Rose/Lou calls.

LT: Stick blocks; is alert for possible KC call.

Receivers and Backs

X: Runs comeback route at depth of 18 yards; comes back to 15 yards. First digit (5) = X route.

Z: Runs post route with breaking point at 12 yards. Third digit (8) = Z route.

Y: Runs stick route at depth of 10 to 12 yards. Second digit (3) = Y route.

FB: Checks, alert for gap, KC, Rose/Lou, over, M, or help calls. If not needed for protection, runs angle route.

TB: Checks; alert for gap, KC, Rose/Lou, over, M, or help calls. If not needed, runs stretch route.

QB: Presnap, reads weakside CB; takes 5-step drop, postsnap reads either weak-curl-flat, or strongside LB. If Z has a retreat, CB looks Z to TB. Any other technique, looks Y to FB.

Coaching Points

- The QB emphasizes the brown call in the huddle. This alerts the C for protection mode.

- While making his break, it is important for Z to be ready for the ball; vs. cover 2, X adjusts to run a corner route. Y must read man or zone coverage.

- Trump or Rose/Lou calls are made by the QB at the LOS to protect the four-man side. If two defenders are in the A gaps, the QB will make Rose/Lou calls. The backside back is alert for gap call.

- Backs on help call sit on inside hip of tackle; they do not create help.

- Brown stay protection call keeps the TE in.

- Y is hot receiver off LB blitz.

Jack Johnson

Pickerington High School

Pickerington, Ohio

Check Pass

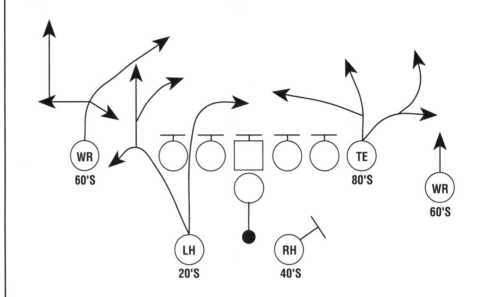

Play Strategy

Coach Johnson's complete series has unlimited short passing potential. This series can be called anywhere on the field. Play calls depend on the kinds of coverages. For example, vs. man coverage with inside leverage on the WR, 61 is called. Versus 8 man front/3 cover with weakside OB stunt, 63 is called. Versus 2 cover/strongside LB stunt or TE not being bumped, 82 is called. Versus 7 or 8 man front with a hard charge from the outside, 21 or 41 may be called.

Player Assignments

Formation: **Split Backs**

Offensive Linemen

The Check Pass is a very simple system used to handle nonread stunting defenses. Line protection involves cut blocking below the waist of the defensive lineman. This technique keeps the defensive linemen's hands down on the 3-step drop play. In an exception, the #4 route is designed as a 5-step pocket protection route.

Receivers and Backs

WR: The 60s series is designed for wideouts. No. 1: O stands for an outcut. No. 2: H stands for hitch. No 3: I stand for slant in. No. 4: O stands for an out and up. With 20, 40, and 80 calls, runs the 4 route.

TE: The 80s series is designed for the tight end. It uses the same route numbers as the WR. With 20, 40, and 60 calls, blocks the same as the line.

LH: The 20s series is designed for the LH. It uses the same route numbers as the WR. With 40, 60, and 80 calls, stays to block.

RH: The 40s series is designed for the RH. It uses the same route numbers as the WR. With 20, 60, and 80 calls, stays to block.

QB: Executes 3-step drop for route numbers 1, 2, and 3. With No. 4 call, takes 5-step drop.

Coaching Points

■ These four-pass routes can be called from the sidelines, checked off by the QB, or signaled by the receiver.

■ To run the four routes, the receivers need to count to four and spell Ohio.

■ Routes 1, 2, and 3 require aggressive blocking below the waist; route-4 blockers stay on their feet and form a pocket.

■ One feature of the series is that the calls can be made with or without a huddle.

■ The most productive series of the check pass package is run out of the pro formation.

■ 40 series (not diagrammed) routes same as 20.

Z Burst

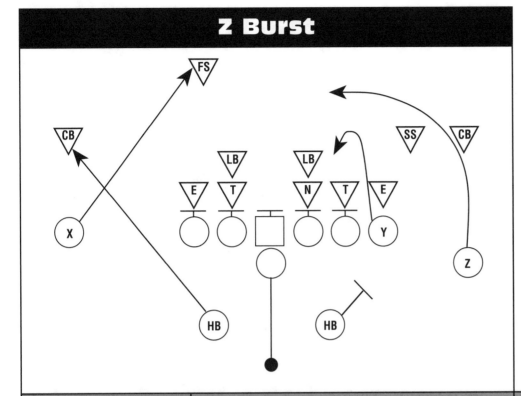

Harry Welch

Canyon High School

Canyon Country,
California

Play Strategy	Player Assignments	Coaching Points

Play Strategy

The Z Burst is a high-scoring pass play that you can run against most coverages, including man. The reads by the two wideouts are effective in all situations and in most coverages. This is a good third-down play. To supplement the running game, this play has also been modified with play action. The defense must prepare to stop the Z Burst, against both dropback and play action.

Player Assignments

Formation: **Split Backs**

Offensive Linemen

Dropback blocking rules are basic. They are simplified to give the QB 3 to 3-1/2 seconds of protection. The offensive linemen rules are *in*, *over*, and *area*. The pass rush lanes are the responsibility of each player from inside to outside.

Receivers and Backs

X: Runs a deep read route. Versus cover 2, drives near CB to end zone.

Y: Releases inside; runs a curl route at 8 yards.

Z: Runs a burst route. Versus cover 2, runs 15 yards straight at the CB, bends at 20 yards, and runs straight to the opposite sideline.

LH: Runs wide deep circle route to keep CB on X side in his zone.

RH: Provides maximum protection to his side and/or safety valve releases.

QB: Takes a 7 to 9 step drop. If in play action, takes a deeper drop.

Coaching Points

■ The TE curl route opens a large vertical zone between the LB and defensive secondary.

■ Z is taught that bending the route is a speed turn.

■ Presnap, the QB reads the secondary. His primary receiver is Z. He is thrown to in all man and cover 2 situations.

■ QB reads FS, if FS drops deep with X, the ball is thrown to Z as if throwing to a deep-in route lead. This leads Z to the opposite sideline.

■ If the FS steps up to help on Z, the ball is thrown to X just over the FS's head.

87

Bob McQueen

Temple High School

Temple, Texas

Trey Left Fan Right 94 Y Choice

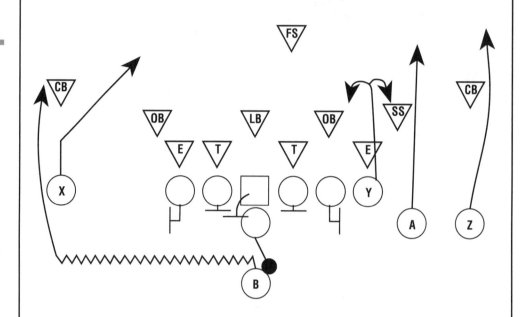

Play Strategy	Player Assignments	Coaching Points

Play Strategy

This has big-play potential. Coach McQueen doesn't hesitate to call this play in second-and-long or third-and-long situations. X and B motion puts pressure on the CB, who has two receivers to cover. There is little help from the FS, who is aligned on the trips side. During the last 2 seasons, the play has averaged 24 yards per catch for Coach McQueen's team.

Player Assignments

Formation: **Trips**

Offensive Linemen

The 5-Step dropback pass protection package is the same for all five linemen. First, each lineman base blocks man on and protects the area around. Second, each lineman is responsible for protecting the inside gap; C helps right or left.

Receivers and Backs

X: Runs 3-step slant route, looks for ball on the break.

Z: Runs clear route to take the CB out of his zone area.

Y: Releases outside; runs choice route at 10 yards.

A: Runs clear route on the hashmark to take defender out of his zone area.

B: Goes in motion weak side; runs clear route.

QB: Takes a 5-step drop; reads X slant route to Y choice route.

Coaching Points

■ The defense is spread horizontally with trips to the wide side and X split to the short side.

■ Receivers running the clear route must sell the deep pass so coverage reacts.

■ B, in motion, runs the bottom of the field numbers and always looks for the ball to be thrown his way.

■ QB reads Will LB for the X slant route; if covered, looks back to TE on choice route.

20 Read

Don Read

University of Montana

Missoula, Montana

Big Sky Conference
(1AA)

Play Strategy	Player Assignments	Coaching Points

Play Strategy

This simple timing pass play is used to set up the run. The pass play 20 Read is effective from the –20 to the +20 yardline area. The effectiveness of this play depends on how quickly the backside SE reads the coverage. He must determine whether the defense is playing zone, man, or roll up. By reading the CB, the playside SE and SB run complementary routes. The QB makes the appropriate read and throws. If the FS bites on the flag route, the drag route may open for the backside SE.

Player Assignments

Formation: **Double Slot**

Offensive Linemen

ONT: Blocks #1 (DE).

ONG: Zone blocks #2 and #3.

C: Zone blocks #2 and #3.

OFG: Zone blocks #2 and #3.

OFT: Zone blocks #2 and #3.

Receivers and Backs

BSSE: Runs drag through middle zone 10 to 20 yards deep.

BSSB: Blocks #1 (DE).

ONSE: Reads near CB on release. If CB deepens, runs out route. If CB flattens or rolls up, runs flag route.

ONSB: Reads CB on release. If CB deepens, runs flag route. If CB flattens or rolls up, runs out route.

RB: Checks backside blitz from alley defender. Serves as general protector for the QB.

QB: Takes 3-step drop, reading playside CB. Throws to playside SE on out route if the CB softens. Throws to playside SE on flag route if the CB rolls up or flattens. If flag route is to be thrown, switches from 3 steps to 5.

Coaching Points

■ The QB is protected by zone line blocking. This blocking technique allows the QB to concentrate on his CB read as he drops to throw.

■ The QB gets the ball in throwing position (up to the top of his numbers) on drop, in case the out pattern needs to be thrown.

■ If the called play is left and the QB is right handed, make sure his right foot is planted well and the hip opened partially to the LOS on the final step. This insures a quick delivery.

■ If using a sprint out attack, the QB must be ready to throw on the third step. This positions him behind the guard.

■ The distance between the two outside receivers, the SE and SB, should be no less than 10 yards.

■ Although great separation between the two receivers is preferred, this depends on the arm strength of the QB.

Jeff Scurran

Sabino High School

Tucson, Arizona

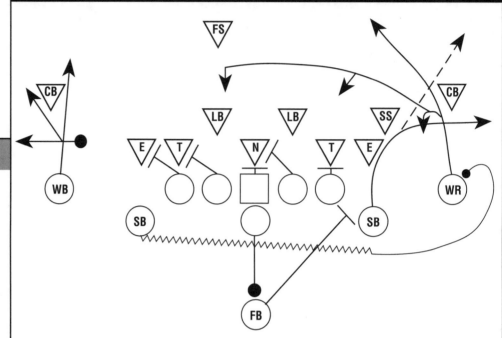

Gangster Pass Right: Curl & Out

Play Strategy

The blocking scheme used for the Gangster Pass is a game decision. With so many reads available, the Gangster Pass may be thrown on any down or distance. Prior to the snap, defenses should be balanced. Then, after motion across the formation, defenses are forced to adjust. The sideline reads of Coach Scurran help the on-field reads of the QB.

Player Assignments

Formation: Double Slot

Offensive Linemen

Three blocking schemes: (a) gangster, (b) slide, and (c) bandit.

RT: (a) Blocks first down man inside DE, (b) blocks playside DE, and (c) blocks gap to DG.

RG: (a) Blocks second down man inside DE, (b) blocks frontside #2, and (c) blocks gap to frontside.

C: (a) Blocks Nose to backside A, (b) blocks frontside A to Nose, and (c) blocks gap to A frontside.

LG: (a) Blocks A gap to backside B, (b) blocks Nose to backside B, and (c) blocks Nose to A playside.

LT: (a) Blocks B gap to backside C, (b) blocks offside DE, and (c) blocks B gap playside.

Receivers and Backs

PSWR: Sprints downfield; reads playside LB: (1) If LB backpedals to curl or steps to cut off line of pattern, WR takes window #1 at 11 yards; (2) if LB opens hip and sprints to cut off line of pattern, WR rounds pattern at 14 yards to window #2; (3) if another LB appears playside by rotating over, WR cuts to #2 and takes window #3; and (4) if FS doesn't go to deep middle and appears in curl zone, WR sprints to post.

PLSB: Reads inside LB for hot route. If no blitz, rounds corner at 7 yards and runs a 12-yard Banana Out route.

BSSB: Goes in motion across formation. After snap, sprints 15 yards outside of PST on LOS. Runs a swing route.

BSWR: Checks CB's position and depth for outside automatics.

FB: (a) Blocks frontside DE, (b) blocks backside LB, and (c) blocks backside DG.

QB: Progressive reads: (a) Presnap, reads coverage of BSWR for automatics. (b) Before motion, checks for position of LBs, SS, FS, and CB. (c) During motion, looks for inside LB blitz and/or jams on PSWR. (d) On dropback, has two choices: if inside LB blitzes, throws to PSSB; if SS stays back or OLB blitzes, throws to PSSB. (e) No blitzes, checks FS for robber and PSWR post route. If not, reads PSWR for curl route on window openings. (f) Coverage jammed inside, reads PSSB route on SS to outside. (g) All coverage dropped off, throws swing route to BSSB.

Coaching Points

- While running the curl route, the PSWR understands that the OLB is #3, the inside LB is #2, and the FS is #4.

- If the PSSB is covered in man or the SS cuts under, the out route pattern is extended to 17 yards.

- After turning up field, it is important that the BSSB squares his shoulders and looks for ball.

- The BSWR and QB read the CB's alignment for four options: (1) if the CB is inside-tight, the WR runs the fade route; (2) if the CB is outside-tight, the WR runs the fly route; (3) if the CB is inside-loose, the WR runs the quick out route; and (4) if the CB is outside-loose, the WR runs the hitch route.

Part III

Special Plays

The first two parts of *Football's Best Offensive Playbook* provided an excellent assortment of traditional plays, run from standard formations. The types of plays you'll call more than 95% of the time.

In this section we'll add to the other 1% to 5% of your play list. These are the innovative—some would say wacky—plays that you always suspect you'll need in a big game and crucial situation. They're also the type of plays that brings out the kid in all of us. Didn't we all run a flea flicker back in our weekend pick-up games with the neighborhood kids? The play looked so perfect drawn up in a muddy patch in the huddle. And it worked! Well, about 10% of the time—but when it did work it was somehow more magical than other scoring plays.

The veteran coaches who contributed to this part of the book have taken those youth-inspired trick plays and made them work. The reverses, throwbacks, and other deceptive plays you'll find here are excellent calls against cheating and over-pursuing defenses. And they are a great surprise to a defense that is lulled to sleep after a series of short-yardage, running plays. A quick 6! These

plays are favorites of everyone—fans, media, and players. Coaches like them, too (unless they backfire or an opponent runs one to score). Two of the book's best special plays are Pete Levine's 344 Crazy (p. 117) and Bennie Edens' Statue of Liberty (p. 121).

Officials don't always appreciate the trickery. For example, Nebraska's score off of the fumblerooski play in the 1984 Orange Bowl led to a ban on this particular form of high jinx. Now every offensive lineman who dreamed of scooping the hidden ball off the turf and rambling across the goal line for the winning score must resign himself to the fact that such opportunities will arise only when a teammate fumbles. His number will no longer be called in the huddle.

Please understand if the diagrams for the following plays are a bit confusing. And believe me when I tell you that the plays are illustrated as neatly as possible; in truth, they look much less orderly when executed. The coaches' descriptions should clarify any questions you have. If not, write to the coach whose play is of interest. And be sure to thank him ahead of time for adding a new dimension to your playbook.

Play List

Coach	Play	Formation
Reverses		
Terry Donahue	Z Reverse	I
Dexter Wood	Right 22 Reverse at 9	I
Bob Deter	Belly 58 Reverse	I
Max Hawk	26 Reverse	Wing-T
Mike Price	316 Double Reverse Pass	One-Back
Throwbacks		
Jim Sweeney	Z Reverse Throwback to QB	I
Brian O'Reilly	121 Waggle Throwback	Wing-T
Jim Ragland	Cowboy Under Left	Split Backs
PATs		
Pete Levine	344 Crazy	Bone
Mac Barousse	Woody One	PAT
Bruce Reynolds	Special Left Pull	FG
Trick Plays		
Nick Hyder	Flea Flicker Left	Pro
Bennie Edens	Z Statue Left	Trips

Z Reverse

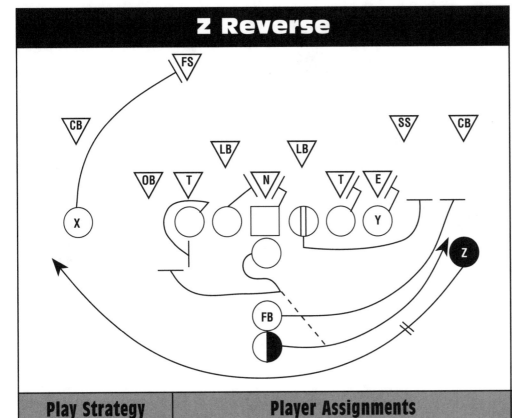

Terry Donahue

University of California at Los Angeles

Los Angeles, California

Pac-10 Conference (1A)

Play Strategy	Player Assignments	Coaching Points

Play Strategy

You'll have your best success with this play when facing a soft wide OB or a reduced defense on the weak side. The Z reverse tries to achieve a moment where the QB and BST (relative to the sweep fake) have the backside penetrators engulfed. The more overshifted the defense is to the strong side, the better to run the play. The play is a companion play to the sweep.

Player Assignments

Formation: **I-Formation**

Offensive Linemen

PST: Sweep blocks man on.

PSG: Pulls playside around the block of TE; blocks first defender to show.

C: Scoop blocks Nose with BSG.

BSG: Scoop blocks Nose with C.

BST: If there are two backside defenders, initiates sweep block. Moves inside until defender is out of vision, peels around, and keeps defender out of pursuit.

Receivers and Backs

X: Blocks the first safety to the inside.

Y: Reach blocks man on.

Z: Runs backside path behind the TB, receives handoff from the TB, sprints around peel blocks, follows the escort and blocks of the C and BSG.

FB: Runs playside; blocks the SS.

TB: Runs playside, receives toss from QB, hands off to Z, and continues on same path.

QB: Reverse pivots, toss to TB, runs backside, and positions himself to block defender assigned to contain.

Coaching Points

- If only one LOS defender is outside of the BST after he initiates the sweep block, the BST does not peel block.

- The QB is to keep the play from going into pressure from either side. In a seven-man front, a wide OB is considered pressure.

- The key to running this play is to block the sweep first.

91

Dexter Wood

Marietta High School

Marietta, Georgia

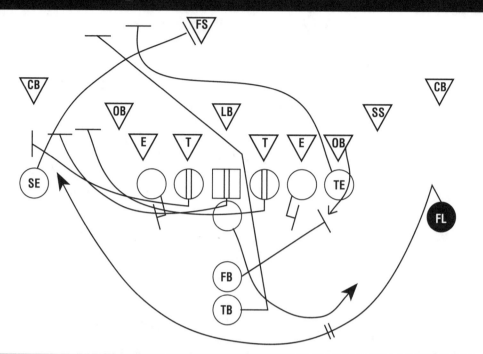

Right 22 Reverse at 9

Play Strategy

In normal situations, this is a favorite first- or second-down call. Coach Wood runs the 22 Draw to establish the inside running game, to keep the defense honest, and before running the reverse. After studying the DE and the defensive pressure from the weak side, it is almost certain that the play will be called.

Player Assignments

Formation: **I-Formation**

Offensive Linemen

LT: Shows 22 draw pass block, gets depth, and invites DE to pass rush.

LG: Holds 1 count pass block; pulls under LT's block to kickout containment.

C: Holds 1 count pass block; pulls down LOS to block downfield.

RG: Holds 1 count pass block, pulls down LOS, and looks to seal backside.

RT: Pass blocks; shows 22 draw.

Receivers and Backs

SE: Releases inside, runs slant route, and blocks FS.

TE: Releases inside; blocks downfield ahead of BC.

FL: Takes hitch step, aims toward TB's feet (7 yards depth), and receives handoff from QB. Sprints toward CB; reads the blocks of C and the pulling guards.

FB: Blocks backside DE.

TB: Fakes 22 draw; runs downfield to block.

QB: Fakes 22 draw with TB, gets depth, and brings ball to FL for the exchange. Runs away from playside.

Coaching Points

■ Prior to pulling, a 1-count hold by both guards and the C is necessary to slow pass rush and to arrive at the POA on time with the FL reverse.

■ Regardless of the TB's fake inside, the timing of the ball exchange between the QB and FL is critical.

■ The fake must hold the two inside LBs so they don't recognize the reverse.

Belly 58 Reverse

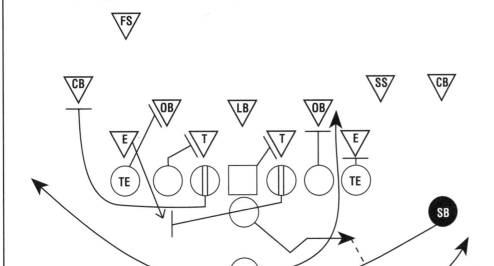

Bob Deter

Sheridan High School

Englewood, Colorado

Play Strategy	Player Assignments	Coaching Points

Play Strategy

You can use the Belly 58 Reverse effectively in numerous down/distance situations. Coach Deter calls this play in any formation that employs a flanker, SE, or double tight. This play is used against hard pursuing defenses that do not leave anyone on the backside to contain. Even if the DE or OLB stay home, the pulling guards are there to make the blocks. It is a helpful strategy to establish the belly option before running this play. The play, along with pass options, has been extremely good for Coach Deter over the years.

Player Assignments

Formation: **I-Formation**

Offensive Linemen

LT: Down blocks for pulling LG.

LG: Pulls left; blocks CB.

C: Blocks for pulling RG.

RG: Pulls left; blocks EMOL.

RT: Base blocks defender on or over.

Receivers and Backs

LE: Releases inside to block near LB.

RE: Base blocks defender on.

FB: Steps out; runs track for belly option.

TB: Runs the pitch track for belly option; gains depth.

QB: Fronts out, rides belly fake with FB, and then pitches back to SB going opposite.

SB: Receives pitch from the QB sprinting opposite; reads blocks of pulling guards.

Coaching Points

■ The QB, FB, and TB execute the play as if they were running the base belly option series.

■ Both pulling guards fire out as if involved in play action pass blocking. They must delay pulling for 1-1/2 to 2 seconds to execute the timing of the SB at the POA.

■ With the exception of the pulling guards, all linemen use influence blocks so that the defense is sold on the original play action or on the outside belly.

93

Max Hawk

Yankton High School

Yankton, South Dakota

26 Reverse

Play Strategy	**Player Assignments**	**Coaching Points**

Play Strategy

In the Wing-T offense, this is an excellent play in long-yardage situations. This play should always be run to the short side, as defenses tend to expect the power off-tackle play on the wide side. The play can be run successfully vs. 4-4, 4-3, and split 6. As the threat of running the bootleg pass helps to keep the defense backed up, the 26 Reverse is a good play to use as a counter.

Player Assignments

Formation: **Wing-T**

Offensive Linemen

RT: Drive blocks DT.

RG: Pulls left; blocks EMOL out.

C: Blocks Nose away from POA.

LG: Blocks first defender outside of C.

LT: Blocks second defender outside of C.

Receivers and Backs

SE: Releases downfield to stalk block CB.

TE: Pulls left, turns up through hole, and looks to block FS.

FB: Runs at inside leg of RG; blocks first defender outside C.

HB: Takes handoff from QB, hands back inside to WB, and continues upfield.

QB: Opens to HB, hands off, and fakes bootleg wide.

WB: Delays 1 count, follows the TE, takes an inside handoff from HB, and turns upfield at POA.

Coaching Points

- Using good faking technique, the QB must make the DE think it is a bootleg play.

- After making a handoff to the WB, the HB may engage the DE. If not, he runs upfield.

- The pulling TE's block on the FS is vital to breaking the play wide open.

- The pulling RG's block on the DE is key to opening up the POA for the TE and WB.

316 Double Reverse Pass

Mike Price

Washington State University

Pullman, Washington

Pac-10 Conference (1A)

Play Strategy	Player Assignments	Coaching Points

Play Strategy

Coach Price likes to use the Double Reverse Pass on the first play of the game when defenses aren't expecting it. The play is run off their #1 running play and they want the safeties to bite on the run. Versus 3-deep zone, X runs a crack corner route.

Player Assignments

Formation: **One-Back**

Offensive Linemen

Block regular 16 zone rules:

ST: If covered, blocks defender on. If uncovered, works a scoop combination with SG from the down defensive lineman to the strongside LB.

SG: If covered, blocks defender on. If uncovered, works a scoop combination with ST from the down defensive lineman to the strongside LB.

C: If covered, blocks defender on. Works a scoop block with SG from the Nose and strongside LB. If uncovered, steps playside and looks to help QG.

QG: If covered, blocks the defender on. If uncovered, looks to help the QT secure the down defensive lineman and hinge blocks to help against backside pressure.

QT: Blocks the defender on.

Receivers and Backs

TE: Blocks the defender on; protects inside gap.

X: Fakes stalk block; releases deep.

Z: Runs reverse path to a point 7 yards deep for the mesh point of the handoff. Takes handoff, gains depth to a point 10 yards deep, runs for 4 or 5 steps, and sets up to throw.

SR: Tightens split to 4 yards from tackle. Takes handoff from QB at about 5 yards. Deepens slightly and hands ball to Z. Protects backside looking for CB chasing Z.

RB: Fakes zone weak; secures the corner.

QB: Fakes zone weak, hands ball to SR, turns back, and secures the throw.

Coaching Points

■ Play success depends on the aggressive and sustained blocking of the line, especially the TE's block.

■ The TE cannot get beaten to the inside. The SR must be in position to pick off the CB if he chases.

■ The SG must be alert for the LB running through the strong A gap. The C must also be on the alert for the LB running through.

■ It is the responsibility of the QT and the RB to secure the corner.

■ Z holds the key to selling the defense that a play is being run. After the handoff, he must tuck the ball away like a running back. On the fourth or fifth step, he sets up and throws quickly to X. If X is covered, he runs or throws the ball away.

95

Jim Sweeney

Fresno State University

Fresno, California

Western Conference
(1A)

Z Reverse Throwback to QB

Play Strategy

Coach Sweeney's philosophy includes running special plays when the defense least expects it. A reverse by itself is a tough play to defend, but when a throwback pass to the QB is added, it becomes even more difficult. For this play to be successful, the QB must be open to receive the pass.

Player Assignments

Formation: **I-Formation**

Offensive Linemen

PST: Short sets to block man on; with no one on, sets to block first man inside.

PSG: Sets to block man on; with no one on, sets to block with C.

C: Sets to block man on; with no one on, checks middle LB to offside.

OFG: Sets to block man on; with no one on, sets off double read LBs.

OFT: Sets to block man on; with no one on, sets to block first man outside.

Receivers and Backs

SE: Drives CB off, breaks, and runs deep post route.

TE: Releases crossfield; runs past original alignment of FS.

FL: Runs reverse course, takes pitch from QB, stays wide, stretches perimeter as far as possible, pulls up, and throws back to QB.

FB: Blocks EMOL, loses contact, idles down, starts to drift, and turns upfield to seal off inside.

TB: Fakes strong lead, runs through at onside LB, idles down, starts to drift, turns upfield to seal off inside.

QB: Fakes strong lead to TB, pitches to Z running reverse track, idles down and deepens, wings wide, and looks for pass from Z.

Coaching Points

■ The offensive line must maintain contact to avoid defensive penetration.

■ As the TE runs his crossing route, he needs to occupy and catch the attention of the FS.

■ Both the FB and TB have to be good actors so they can be in a position to seal off the inside.

■ Z's pass to the QB is a throwback, not a downfield pass.

121 Waggle Throwback

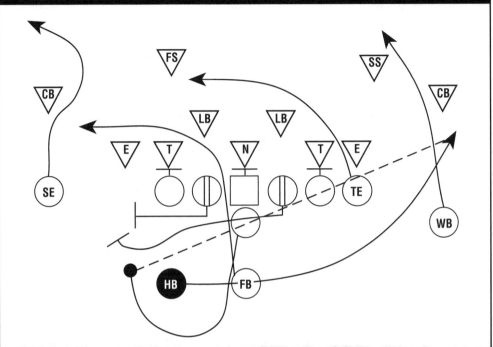

Brian O'Reilly

Pinkerton Academy

Derry, New Hampshire

Play Strategy	Player Assignments	Coaching Points

Play Strategy

This misdirection play is good on fourth down and is an excellent scoring play from inside the 25-yard line. The play is used sparingly but has big-play potential. The defensive secondary can be caught reacting to the base waggle. If HB is not open, QB still has reads on the waggle side.

Player Assignments

Formation: **Wing-T**

Offensive Linemen

RT: Area blocks; looks to block DT.

RG: Pulls backside, gets depth, and blocks the flank.

C: Area blocks; looks to block Nose.

LG: Pulls backside; blocks first defender outside of LT.

LT: Area blocks; looks to block DT.

Receivers and Backs

SE: Runs corner route to occupy the CB or FS.

TE: Runs drag route to draw the attention of the LBs.

WB: Runs post route to occupy the SS or CB.

FB: Dives backside gap between C/LG; releases into the flat.

HB: Fakes sweep, fakes a block on DE, and runs flare route.

QB: Reverse pivots, runs waggle, pulls up, and throws back to HB.

Coaching Points

- The QB concentrates on making a ball fake to the HB. The ball is placed on hip while he is threatening the flank.

- If the LB blitzes, the FB blocks him and avoids the flat.

- Throughout the blocking area, the OTs must block any defender coming through.

- To force the defense to react, the SE, TE, and WB sell the idea that they are going to be the receiver.

- The throwback pass to the HB is a forward pass downfield.

Jim Ragland

Tennessee Tech University

Cookeville, Tennessee

Ohio Valley Conference (1AA)

Cowboy Under Left

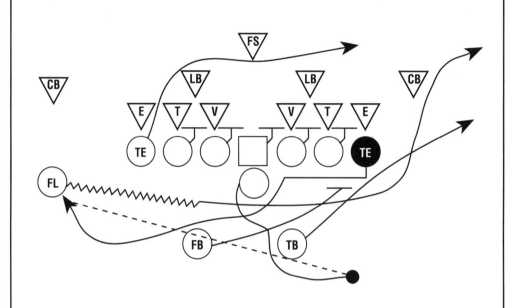

Play Strategy

This special play is used in goal-line or 2-point situations. The situation dictates that a defense will be in some type of goal-line scheme. (Specific goal-line defenses are used within the 5-yard line.) The double tight end formation pressures the defense to be balanced, and a running motion across the formation into the deep corner forces the secondary to make immediate on-field adjustments. When there is a strong backside rush, the PSTE is left alone, which enables him to score. If necessary, the QB can also throw playside to the TB in the flat or to the FL in the deep corner.

Player Assignments

Formation: **Split Backs**

Offensive Linemen (2 Splits)

PST: Reach blocks playside.

PSG: Reach blocks playside.

C: Reach blocks playside.

BSG: Turn blocks backside.

BST: Turn blocks backside.

Receivers and Backs

BSTE: Releases inside and runs drag route all the way across the formation, at a depth of 8 to 10 yards.

FL: Comes in motion across the formation; runs flag route into the corner of the end zone.

PSTE: Dropsteps and runs flat behind the LOS until behind the BSG. Gets depth.

FB: Blocks first defender outside the PST.

TB: Releases playside into the flat at a depth of 6 yards.

QB: Reverses out, fakes to FB, goes to a depth of 9 yards, and sets up behind the PST.

Coaching Points

■ PSTE is the primary receiver. As quickly as possible, he runs flat behind the LOS at a depth of 7 yards. It is essential that his depth is correct so that he coordinates with the QB's depth of 9 yards.

■ The timing of the pass is critical. The QB throws the ball over the PSTE's inside shoulder.

■ The offensive line must stop penetration so that the PSTE can go behind the LOS without rerouting.

344 Crazy

Pete Levine

Mullen Prep

Lakewood, Colorado

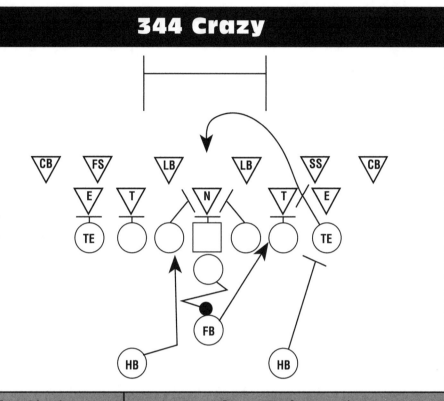

| Play Strategy | Player Assignments | Coaching Points |

Play Strategy

Over the years, Coach Levine has used this play action goal-line play with his wishbone offense. The 344 Crazy is used only as a 2-point conversion play. By faking dive right and faking counter-dive left, both safeties hold. In a goal-line situation, the inside LBs must honor the two backs faking both sides. The RH load block and left TE base block help to hold off the containment of the DEs.

Player Assignments

Formation: **Bone**

Offensive Linemen

This wishbone play is run with double TEs. It utilizes line splits of 3 feet from the Gs, Ts, and LE. The RE is split 4 feet so he can escape from the LOS. The linemen base block.

Receivers and Backs

RE: The RE releases inside or outside; runs to end line under the goal post.

LE: Base blocks.

RH: Load blocks on the DE who is aligned over the RE.

FB: Runs track at the outside leg of RG; fakes the dive.

LH: Runs track at inside leg of LG: fakes the counterdive.

QB: Opens up right, fakes the FB dive, spins, and fakes the counterdive with his back to the LOS. Flips the ball backward over his head.

Coaching Points

■ Players are to keep in mind that they are running a normal wishbone counterplay.

■ After making fakes to the FB and LH, with his back to the LOS, the QB flips the ball backward over his head to the RE.

■ It is the RE's responsibility to be on the end line. He positions himself under the goal post in a direct line with the QB. He watches and waits for the lob pass.

■ Both backs carry out their fakes to draw the attention of the safeties.

Mac Barousse

Carencro High School

Lafayette, Louisiana

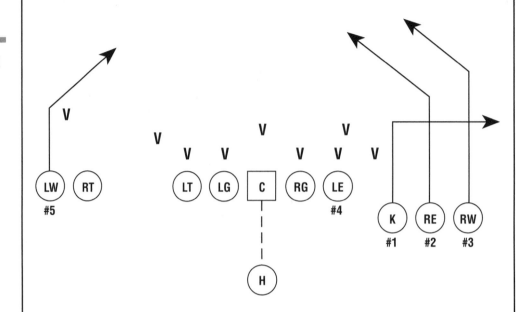

Woody One

Play Strategy

Usually the QB has a call from the sideline. Since every receiver is numbered, the combination of routes is unlimited. As diagrammed, Woody One has #1 (K) as the primary receiver. Three different formations with pass routes confuse any defense. Coach Barousse and his special teams coach, Tony Courville, believe that defenses are forced to prepare and practice when meeting their team.

Player Assignments

Formation: **PAT**

Swinging Gate Alignment

LE, LT, LG, RG, and RT stand shoulder to shoulder 10 yards to the left of the C on the LOS.

RE: Wide right on LOS.

LW: In the gap behind the RG and RT.

RW: In the slot between the C and RE.

Holder and kicker are in normal PAT set.

Woody Formation Alignment

LW: Wide left (#5).

RT: Wide left, inside of LW.

C: Over the ball.

LT: Second man left of C.

LG: First man left of C.

RG: First man right of C.

LE: Second man right of C (#4).

K: Splits right; first inside receiver next to RE (#1).

RE: Splits right, second inside receiver between K and RW (#2).

RW: Splits right; outside receiver next to RE (#3).

Coaching Points

- Start with the swinging gate alignment to see how the defense adjusts to the formation.

- If there is no swinging gate play, the team shifts into a regular PAT formation.

- All players are standing except the C. They are taught to remain still.

- If called, the ball is kicked in the PAT formation.

- It is very important for all players to be set for 1 second before the "Woody" call.

- The Woody formation confuses a defense, which has a difficult time making proper adjustments.

Special Left Pull

Bruce Reynolds

William Penn High School

New Castle, Delaware

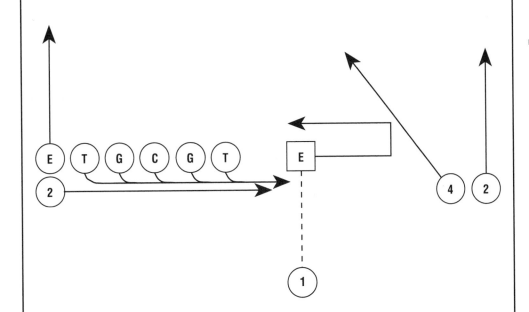

Play Strategy	Player Assignments	Coaching Points

Play Strategy

This surprise play is run on any down, anywhere on the field. This is especially run from –20 yard line to the +20 yard line. The defensive team that huddles and comes out slowly is vulnerable. Coach Reynolds uses this play also for 2-point conversions with a minor modification of routes.

Player Assignments

Formation: **FG**

Offensive Linemen

LT: Turns right and pulls parallel to LOS.

LG: Turns right and pulls parallel to LOS.

C: Turns right and pulls parallel to LOS.

RG: Turns right and pulls parallel to LOS.

RT: Turns right and pulls parallel to LOS.

Receivers and Backs

OFE: Takes over C responsibility. Makes direct snap back to 1-QB; runs parallel to LOS.

2 ONWB: Blocks onside, drives deep upfield, and looks for pass from QB.

2 OFWB: Blocks offside, runs right behind pulling linemen, and looks for pass from QB.

ONE: Drives deep upfield and looks for pass from QB.

4-FB: Releases inside at 45 degrees; looks for pass.

1-QB: Aligns at a depth of 11 yards, scrambles, and looks for open receiver.

Coaching Points

■ It is very hard to predict what the defense will do against this formation.

■ After breaking the huddle, the team lines up immediately and is ready for the play.

■ QB reads presnap to see what coverage the defense has employed. If one of the five potential receivers is not covered, the ball is thrown to him.

■ In running their routes, offside 2-WB, 4-FB, and ONE make a decision to cut on the fifth step.

■ The scrambling of the QB forces the defense to pursue out of lanes. The QB looks for an open receiver.

Nick Hyder

Valdosta High School

Valdosta, Georgia

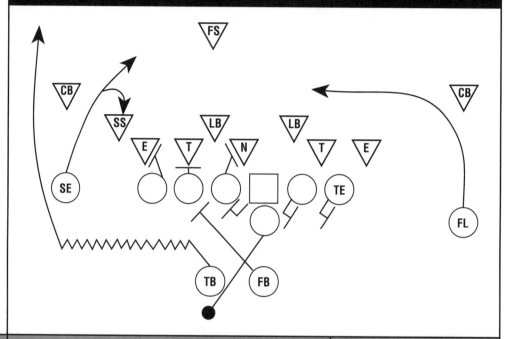

Flea Flicker Left

Play Strategy	Player Assignments	Coaching Points

Play Strategy

This play is good when a first down is needed. It is useful in clutch situations such as a third down and 5 to 12 yards. The unbalanced line provides an element of surprise. The TB motion often catches defenses off guard. Using this same formation, Coach Hyder also runs a double screen pass to the FB or TE (slow rush).

Player Assignments

Formation: **Pro**

Offensive Linemen

The line is unbalanced to the left. It has two tackles opposite the TE on that side.

PST and BST: Both tackle block man on or outside.

PSG: Blocks man on or inside gap.

C: Blocks man on or playside gap.

BSG: Blocks man on or inside gap.

Receivers and Backs

SE: Releases to run post route then stops; curls quickly toward the QB.

TE: Stays to block man on or inside gap.

FL: Releases at the CB; runs drag route across.

FB: Steps playside to check LB blitz.

TB: Goes in motion playside; sprints down the sideline.

QB: QB fronts out; rolls to set up behind PST/PSG gap at depth of 7 yards.

Coaching Points

■ While in motion, the TB puts pressure on the CB, who is aligned on the SE. The timing of each is vital to the play.

■ The QB is taught to read through the SS to find the potential receivers, SE or TB, going long.

■ If in trouble, the QB looks backside for the FL, who is running a drag route.

■ If SE reads man coverage, he will continue to run post route.

Z Statue Left

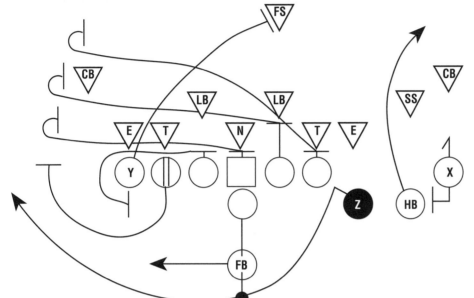

Bennie Edens

Point Loma High School

San Diego, California

Play Strategy	Player Assignments	Coaching Points

Play Strategy

Over the years, Coach Edens has been successful with his version of the statue play in long yardage situations. One of his strategies is to slow down the pass rush everywhere on the field except at the goal line or in short-yardage downs. After studying the DE's pass rush, a strategy is set up to call this play. The play may be run from any formation. It works best to the TE side.

Player Assignments

Formation: **Trips**

Offensive Linemen

SST: Stands up DT, lets him beat him, and then pulls deep left to lead the play.

SG: Sets up pass and watches man on ST; when he passes ST, sprints down LOS to align 2 to 3 yards outside of Y's original position, peels back, and blocks pursuit.

C, QG, and OT: Stand man up, lets him beat them, and sprint 3 (C), 6 (QG), and 9 (OT) yards downfield, 5 yards outside Y's original position. Turn back toward sideline and block their gap.

Receivers and Backs

X: Runs a quick hitch route.

Y: Releases inside, sprints downfield to block FS.

H: Runs a flag route.

FB: Sets up to his left to block right DE. Invites him to rush inside, if DE goes inside FB leads play upfield. If DE stays in outside rush, FB must stay and block DE.

Z: Turns inside and heads for QB's set-up position. Is responsible for picking the ball from the QB; runs away from the LOS. Reading FB's block; turns upfield ASAP. Looks to run behind the downfield wall.

QB: Takes a 5-step drop reading flag route by H. Drops his arm with his palms open; watches Z coming around for the ball.

Coaching Points

- When X runs the hitch route, the hands and eyes are up looking for a pass that should draw the attention of CB.

- H is asked to be good actor. He must convince the DB that he is running a flag route.

- The timing of the QB and Z running the statue play must be precise so that the defense reads pass.

- QB must keep his total concentration on H during the time that Z picks the ball.

Football is a dynamic sport. Teams, players, strategies, training programs, and plays are constantly changing. Everyone's trying to reach the top or become even more dominant. In football, those who try to maintain the status quo suffer. Offensive-minded coaches are never satisfied. Their creative juices flow whether they are designing a new version of an old play or starting fresh. The competition moves ahead.

That's why at the end of the season and after each game, most coaches take a look at their offense and see how they can improve it. Perhaps a certain play or series of plays just wasn't effective. It could have been a personnel problem—key players performing subpar. It might have been that the opposition's defensive scheme was geared to stop it. Or maybe the offensive play-calling was too predictable; the defense was able to anticipate and stop plays based on down-and-distance tendencies. The stakes have never been higher for an offense because the defense keeps crowding the ball. Adding a few new plays or putting in some new wrinkles to plays you already run might re-energize your offense and catch the defense by surprise.

Attention to Details

The 102 plays presented in *Football's Best Offensive Playbook* provide a wide selection of looks and attacks to choose from. The play list offers a variety of formations and blocking schemes for all types of runs and passes. If a play shown isn't run from your base formation, look to see how you might adapt it to your offense. Most of the plays can be run from alternative sets. Even similar plays

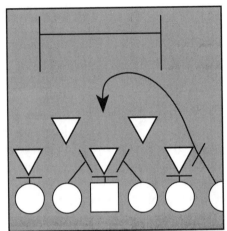

run from the same set can differ in their blocking schemes. The toss sweep plays presented by Bobby Bowden and Tom Osborne, for example, are similar in appearance but not in their blocking assignments. These coaches understand simplicity. They break down every assignment, emphasize technique, and know how to set up a play. Watch out, defense!

The subtleties within each play add to the richness of the book. I began to appreciate these nuances as I compiled the play list. The plays were obviously developed with much thought and attention to detail. That's reflected in the coaches' descriptions and insights accompanying each play diagram.

The book is also a lesson in coaches' use of terms and symbols. If you weren't fluent in football coaching lingo before you opened the book, you should be by the time you've reached this page. Offensive football talk is not a foreign language, but it's close. It's the language of those who coach the most intricate and exciting part of football—offense. Once you grasp the jargon, you're much better able to understand and analyze the variety of plays and judge their pluses, minuses, similarities, and differences.

Football's Best Offensive Playbook should add to your football education, no matter how veteran a coach, player, or fan. The coaches who were kind enough to submit plays to this book are masters of their craft. Their commitment as students of the game has helped them rise to the top of the football coaching profession. They learned from their mentors through books, videos, clinics, and countless numbers of chalk talks. Their success is not a matter of luck—it's a result of their eagerness to learn more about the game and their ability to teach their players.

The attention to detail required in designing an offensive football play—much less an offense—is seldom fully appreciated by those who haven't done it. In no other sport are the movements of so many athletes so interdependent. Along with talent, the play is the tool that drives the offense. Each play provides a means to attack the defense with precise, coordinated actions of 11 men. An offensive playbook is the sheet music for this symphony played out on the football field.

Plays With Style

Coaching football is part science, part art. The artistic side involves such things as interpretation, style, and personality. A coach's personality is often reflected in the plays he prefers. The play reveals something of his true nature, whether he is conservative, cautious, or daring. For example, do you think an introverted, conservative person is going to send in a play like Jim Sweeney's Z Reverse Throwback to QB (p. 114)? Even coaches who have a reserved demeanor, like John Mackovic and LaVell Edwards, prefer a more free-wheeling offensive approach.

Alternatively, many of the most consistently successful coaches subscribe to a run-first philosophy. Power and ball control are their preferences. John McKissick, the winningest football coach in high school history, didn't achieve his remarkable record by being fancy. His famous Blast play (p. 17) has destroyed many defenses over the years. Similarly, Bob Reade has achieved college football coaching's best winning percentage with an offense that features a Wing-T belly series. But when the defense begins overplaying the flow of the option, Bob calls his counterplay (p. 21) and watches his wingback run through a gaping hole.

Whatever style of play they prefer, all successful coaches are pragmatists when it comes to offensive play selection. They run what they think will work best given their personnel, the opponent, and the situation. The coaches in this book think right most of the time.

The Last Play

I hope you enjoyed the book and will find it useful for years to come. If you're a coach, you should have found at least a few plays to add to your own playbook. Feel free to underline and highlight the plays and insights that you find most interesting. And keep your personal copy on a nearby shelf, just in case you get an urge to add a wrinkle or two to your offense.

If you're a player, through studying this book you should have a better understanding of your own team's offense and your opponents' offense. You might want to refer back to notes about positional responsibilities for specific plays if your coach uses them. A smarter player is a better player.

Finally, if you're a football fan—as most of us are—this playbook should help you gain greater appreciation for the strategy that goes into play calling, as well as the many elements that must correspond for a play to run smoothly. Next time your favorite team has the ball, see whether you can figure out the offensive attack, and try to anticipate the coach's play selection.

Putting together *Football's Best Offensive Playbook* has been a lot of fun. For more than a year I have been writing, calling, and faxing coaches for their plays. At times it has been exhilarating, frustrating, and rewarding, but it couldn't have been done without their input. Thanks guys, for sharing. My hope is that your love for the game spreads to all those who read the book.

audible—Verbal change of intended play made in code at LOS by the QB.

backside—Area away from point of attack.

BC—Ball carrier.

BIFOP—Block in front of play.

BOB—Block big on big.

bootleg—Quarterback fakes handoff in one direction and goes opposite direction.

BSCB—Backside cornerback.

BSE—Backside end.

BSG—Backside guard.

BST—Backside tackle.

BSTE—Backside tight end.

BSWR—Backside wide receiver.

CFBP—Cross field blocking point.

COF—Coaching on field.

combo block—Two linemen assigned to block one defender with option for one blocker to block linebacker.

comeback—A pass route in which the receiver turns back toward the passer.

counter—Misdirectional play away from backfield flow.

cross block—At point of attack, tight-end blocks, down, outside tackle blocks out.

cutback—Ball carrier maneuver away from defensive pursuit.

double slot—Formation in which slot backs are lined up in the slot between OT and SE.

double tight—Formation in which each tight end is lined up next to an offensive tackle.

draw—A delayed running play after faking a drop-back pass.

EMOL—End man on line of scrimmage.

even defense—Center is not covered by a defensive lineman.

fold block—At point of attack, outside guard blocks out, outside tackle pulls around outside guard to linebacker.

FSG—Frontside guard.

FST—Frontside tackle.

fullhouse—All four backs in the backfield.

gap—An open defensive space between linemen.

horizontal stretching—Widest possible alignment and release from LOS.

hot receiver—End or back alert for pass if inside linebackers blitz.

I-Formation—FB and TB are positioned in line behind the QB.

in motion—Back moving laterally or in backward direction behind LOS.

influence—An offensive maneuver using a false key to lead defenders away from the POA.

ISO—Identifying a single player to block or attack.

keeper—QB keeps the ball after faking handoff.

lead block—Blocker at head of the ball carrier at point of attack.

LH—Left halfback.

load block—Blocker attacks the defensive end.

log block—Block defender to the inside rather than outside.

LOS—Line of scrimmage.

man coverage—Assigning defender to cover a potential receiver.

north/south—Straight ahead running by the ball carrier toward opponent's goalline.

OB—Outside linebacker.

odd defense—Center is covered by a nose guard.

offside—Area on opposite side of point of attack.

OFG—Offside guard.

OFT—Onside tackle.

ONG—Onside guard.

onside—Area on the side of point of attack.

ONT—Onside tackle.

ONWR—Onside wide receiver.

option—After play begins, QB has option to hand off, run with ball, or pitch.

option block—Blocker takes defender any direction; ball carrier adjusts while running.

PB—Pitchback.

play action—Pass play designed to look like running play.

playside—Area on the side of point of attack.

POA—Point of attack.

pocket—Area behind LOS protected by blockers for the QB.

PSE—Playside end.

PSG—Playside guard.

PST—Playside tackle.

PSTE—Playside tight end.

PSWR—Playside wide receiver.

pulling—Lineman moves laterally to trap or lead.

QG—Quick guard.

QT—Quick tackle.

reverse—BC runs towards sideline opposite of ball flow.

RH—Right halfback.

rule blocking—Predetermined blocking assignments (rules).

screen pass—Pass thrown to receiver or back behind LOS with blockers front.

SG—Strong guard.

shovel pass—BC running behind the LOS receives forward pass.

sight adjustment—End or back alert for pass if defensive backs blitz.

split backs—Running backs are aligned in halfback positions with no fullback.

ST—Strong tackle.

stalk block—Downfield block to occupy defensive secondary.

Statue of Liberty—Play in which back lifts his arm as if to pass but ball is taken by end or back running behind.

strongside—Side where TE is positioned.

technique number—Assigned number corresponding to alignment by down defender.

trap block—Lineman moves laterally to block penetrating defender.

unbalanced line—Four or more offensive linemen on one side.

uncovered—Interior lineman with no defensive lineman on him.

veer—Splitback alignment running some form of triple option.

vertical stretching—Straight upfield as far as possible.

WB—Wingback, positioned just outside and behind the TE.

wedge block—Line moves forward shoulder to shoulder at point of attack.

Xs and Os—Two symbols used to represent offensive plays and defensive strategies.

zone—Block any defender in predetermined area.

zone coverage—Defensive strategy to protect against pass in which specific areas are assigned to defend.

Coaches Index

Coach	Affiliation	Page
College and Pro		
Terry Allen	Northern Iowa	84
Barry Alvarez	Wisconsin	48
Steve Axman	Northern Arizona	96
Bobby Bowden	Florida State	45
Billy Brewer	Mississippi	16
Rich Brooks	Oregon	66
Mack Brown	North Carolina	49
Jim Caldwell	Wake Forest	100
John Cooper	Ohio State	31
Tom Coughlin	Jacksonville (NFL)	99
Herb Deromedi	Central Michigan	50
Gerry DiNardo	Vanderbilt	14
Terry Donahue	UCLA	109
Jim Donnan	Marshall (WV)	91
Spike Dykes	Texas Tech	88
LaVell Edwards	Brigham Young	98
Dennis Erickson	Miami (FL)	90
Gary Gibbs	Oklahoma	15
Keith Gilbertson	California	62
Rocky Hager	North Dakota State	40
Ken Hatfield	Rice	54
Jimmie Keeling	Hardin-Simmons (TX)	79
Roy Kidd	Eastern Kentucky	24
Bill Lewis	Georgia Tech	51

Coach	Affiliation	Page
Sonny Lubick	Colorado State	36
John Mackovic	Texas	97
Bill Mallory	Indiana	87
Glen Mason	Kansas	64
Gary Moeller	Michigan	74
Tom Osborne	Nebraska	47
Mike Price	Washington State	113
Jim Ragland	Tennessee Tech	116
Harold "Tubby" Raymond	Delaware	44
Don Read	Montana	105
Bob Reade	Augustana (IL)	21
Dave Roberts	Northeastern Louisiana	82
Ron Schipper	Central (IA)	63
R.C. Slocum	Texas A & M	27
Bruce Snyder	Arizona State	101
Steve Spurrier	Florida	65
Jim Sweeney	Fresno State	114
Lou Tepper	Illinois	83
Jim Wacker	Minnesota	80
Bob Wagner	Hawaii	55
Jim Walden	Iowa State	52
Frosty Westering	Pacific Lutheran (WA)	86

High School

Mac Barousse	Carencro (Lafayette, LA)	118
Walt Braun	Marysville (MI)	78
Alan Chadwick	Marist (Atlanta, GA)	42
Bob Deter	Sheridan (Englewood, CO)	111
Tom Downing	Wynnewood (OK)	29
Dick Dullaghan	Ben Davis (Indianapolis, IN)	89
Bennie Edens	Point Loma (San Diego, CA)	121

Coach	Affiliation	Page
Terry Ennis	Cascade (Everett, WA)	19
Art Fiore	LaSalle Academy (Providence, RI)	35
Al Fracassa	Brother Rice (Birmingham, MI)	69
Bob Giannunzio	Norway (MI)	20
Tom Grippa	Elder (Cincinnati, OH)	92
John Harvill	Gathersburg (MD)	23
Ronnie Haushalter	Fyffe (AL)	28
Max Hawk	Yankton (SD)	112
Tam Hollingshead	Permian (Odessa, TX)	34
Jerry Horowitz	John F. Kennedy (Bronx, NY)	18
Mike Huard	Puyallup (WA)	67
Nick Hyder	Valdosta (GA)	120
Freddie James	David W. Carter (Dallas, TX)	73
Timothy Jaureguito	South Tahoe (South Lake Tahoe, CA)	43
John Jenkins	Newton (IA)	41
Jack Johnson	Pickerington (OH)	102
Bruce Keith	Sheridan (WY)	53
Joe Kinnan	Manatee (Bradenton, FL)	70
Dennis Kozlowski	Bethel (Hampton, VA)	32
Pete Levine	Mullen Prep (Lakewood, CO)	117
Tom Marcucci	Notre Dame (West Haven, CT)	68
John McKissick	Summerville (SC)	17
Bob McQueen	Temple (TX)	104
Herb Meyer	El Camino (Oceanside, CA)	56
Joe Miller	New Hanover (Wilmington, NC)	85
Chuck Mizerski	Lincoln-Southeast (NB)	46
Tom Moore	Prosser (WA)	22
Jim Nagel	Ashland (OR)	75
Brian O'Reilly	Pinkerton Academy (Derry, NH)	115
Alan Paturzo	Wagner (Staten Island, NY)	95

Coach	Affiliation	Page
Joe Petricca	Palatine (IL)	81
Gil Rector	Lexington (MO)	39
Bruce Reynolds	William Penn (New Castle, DE)	119
Eric Roanhaus	Clovis (NM)	38
Jim Sauls	Leon (Tallahassee, FL)	77
Jerry Schliem	Milton (WI)	93
Jeff Scurran	Sabino (Tucson, AZ)	106
Tony Severino	Rockhurst (Kansas City, MO)	76
Wally Sheets	Washington (Cedar Rapids, IA)	72
Don Soldinger	Miami Southridge (FL)	30
Jack Stark	Shelton (WA)	94
Bob Stone	Joliet Catholic Academy (IL)	26
Chuck Tarbox	Eastside Catholic (Bellevue, WA)	37
Larry Thomas	Baker (LA)	25
Dick Tighe	Webster City (IA)	33
Harry Welch	Canyon (CA)	103
Jarrell Williams	Springdale (AR)	57
Dexter Wood	Marietta (GA)	110
Rich Zinanni	Bishop McNamara (Kankakee, IL)	71

Dee Hawkes began his coaching career assisting Jack Elway (now Pro Scout for the Denver Broncos) at Port Angeles High School in Washington. In 29 subsequent years, Hawkes held four head coaching positions, including stints at Department of Defense schools in Japan and Germany and 18 years at Bothell High School (Washington). In addition, he has extensive experience as a football camp director and motivational speaker.

Although he is no longer a coach, Dee remains committed to prep football as a regular contributor to newspaper and magazine columns and as an analyst for cable TV and radio broadcasts. He has also authored a book on Washington state high school football. Dee is president of the King County Chapter of the National Football Foundation and Hall of Fame and is a member of the American Football Coaches Association and Washington State Coaches Association. In his spare time he enjoys traveling, the theater, and writing. Dee and his family reside in Bothell, Washington.

Coach **Frosty Westering** (left) and **Dee Hawkes**
(Photo by David Hawkes)

You'll find
other outstanding
football resources at

www.HumanKinetics.com

In the U.S. call

1-800-747-4457

Australia 08 8277 1555
Canada 1-800-465-7301
Europe .... +44 (0) 113 255 5665
New Zealand 09-523-3462

 HUMAN KINETICS
The Information Leader in Physical Activity
P.O. Box 5076 • Champaign, IL 61825-5076 USA